GREEK-ENGLISH
ENGLISH-GREEK

DICTIONARY
AND
PHRASEBOOK

Tom Stone

HIPPOCRENE BOOKS
New York

Copyright©1998 Tom Stone

All rights reserved.

For information, address:
HIPPOCRENE BOOKS, INC.
171 Madison Avenue
New York, NY 10016

Cataloging-in-Publication Data available from the Library of Congress

ISBN 0-7818-0635-6

Printed in the United States of America

CONTENTS

Preface	5
Introduction	7
A Very Basic Grammar	11
The Greek Alphabet	17
GREEK-ENGLISH DICTIONARY	19
ENGLISH-GREEK DICTIONARY	75
GREEK PHRASEBOOK	147
Further Reading	259
Maps	260

PREFACE

This is a very basic guide to communicating in modern Greek. Its easy-to-use phonetic system and rudimentary phrases are focused on making your needs quickly understood, with all of the subtle complexities of the language politely put aside for another day. Fortunately, the Greeks are highly appreciative of *any* attempt to speak their language and will fill in all of your grammatical gaps with great gusto, no matter how much you may mangle things.

A Greek-English dictionary has been provided to help the Greeks find words they might want to say to you, and the subsequent English-Greek Dictionary contains a multitude of basic everyday words, including some that might be handy should romance become part of the visit.

📖

- The Greeks call themselves **Helliness** (**El**leeness) and have proudly done so since about 2000 B.C., when a Greek-speaking people of that name, the Hellenes, first arrived in the north of the country.
- We call them "Greeks" because this is what the Romans called them, taking the name from a tribe of Hellenes known as the Graecii which founded a colony on the Italian coast in the 8th century B.C.
- Thus the Greeks call their country **Ellada.** (El**lah**dha).
- Their language is known as **Ellinika** (Elleen**i**ka).
- A male Greek is called a **Ellinas** (El**lee**nas).
- A female Greek is a **Ellinida** (Ellee**nee**dha).
- The adjective for an object whose gender is neuter (this includes a child) is **elliniko** (elleen**i**ko).

- Finally, the city of Istanbul will forever be known in Greece by its original Byzantine Christian name, "Constantinople" (Konstantinopolis).
- It is also know simply as "Ee **Polis**" - "The City".

INTRODUCTION

The Greek-speaking people who called themselves "Hellenes" and arrived in the north of the country in approximately 2000 B.C. were invaders into territory already occupied by Neolithic farming communities from Asia. These had first crossed the Bosphorus c. 7500 B.C. and spread throughout the mainland and the islands, including Crete, over the next five millennia. They were peaceful and probably matrilineal cultures who had no need to erect the walled citadels so identified in our minds with ancient Greece. The latter were built by a branch of the invading Hellenes called Achaeans, who moved south and became known as Mycenaeans, replacing the original Neolithic culture with a war-like patriarchal one that produced most of Greece's heroic legends, many associated with the Trojan War. A subsequent invasion, c. 1200-1100 B.C. by another Greek-speaking people, the Dorians, plunged the country into its Dark Ages, which lasted until c. 750-700, about the time that the works of Homer were first written down.

The period c. 800 to 500 B.C., saw the development of the Greek city-state, most importantly in Corinth, Athens and Sparta., and the establishment of colonies throughout the Mediterranean area from Spain to the Black Sea, north Africa and the present-day Middle East. Contacts with the civilizations of Persia and Lydia through the Greek colonies of Ionia (on the present-day Aegean coast of Turkey) stimulated a growth in the arts and in philosophy that would reach its fullest expression in 5th-century Athens and the Golden Age of Classical Greece.

This magnificent flowering of Athenian culture which produced not only the first democratic state but some of mankind's finest achievements in philosophy, the sciences, and the arts was engendered by an Athenian victory over the Persians at Salamis in 480 B.C., which seemingly made Athens the supreme power in

However, the culture of Greece had resurfaced in a most extraordinary manner as the heart and soul of the great Byzantine empire, informing its arts, politics and religion and being the repository of those all of those works of Classical Greece which would - after the sack of Constantinople by the Ottoman Turks in 1453 - pour forth into Western Europe as the principal contributing factor in that flowering of humanism known as the Renaissance.

In both the Byzantine and Ottoman empires, mainland Greece's major city became Thessaloniki, linked to Rome and Byzantine by the Roman-built Via Egnatia and also easily reached from Constantinople - subsequently named Istanbul by Ataturk in 1930 - through the Dardenelles. Thessaloniki became the second major city of both of these empires and produced two of Orthodox Christianity's greatest saints, Cyril and Methodius, who devised the Cyrillic alphabet and translated the Bible into Slavic. It was also the birthplace of Kemal Mustafa, later known as Ataturk, who would preside over the retrenchment of the Ottoman Empire into modern-day Turkey.

Ottoman rule in Greece lasted almost 400 years, from 1456-1830, and made an indelible mark on the country's language, culture (particularly its music) and cuisine, while at the same time allowing Greeks a precious religious freedom that preserved their national identity and ironically led to their successful uprising against the Turks in 1821-1830. In 1834, the hot and dusty little town of Athens was named the capitol of the newly-formed Kingdom of Greece, which had been created by the Triple Alliance of Britain, Russian and France with the 17-year-old Otto I of Bavaria as monarch.

In 1913, with the above-mentioned territories of Epirus, Macedonia and Crete added to the areas already liberated, Greece assumed virtually the size and shape it has today. In 1923, following the misguided Greco-Turkish War, Greece lost eastern Thrace and Smyrna (Izmir), the toehold it had had on Asia Minor since the Dorian invasions in 1200 B.C. As a result, a massive population exchange took place between the two countries as 1.35 million Greeks and 430, 000 Turks were relocated. The final piece of modern-day Greece was added in 1947 when the Italians renounced their claims on the Dodecanese Islands, which they had taken from Turkey in 1912, and ceded them back to their mother country.

The monarchy survived until 1967, when a coup d'etat by Greek army colonels forced the young King Constantine II to flee the country before the CIA-backed coup he was involved in with army generals could take place. In the 1973 the colonels' junta staged a plebiscite abolishing the monarchy and establishing a "republic" with one of the former colonels at its president. In 1974, with the collapse of the junta and the re-establishment of elective democracy, a new plebiscite confirmed the people's rejection of the monarchy.

Given the history of foreign domination over the last 2000 years, it is no wonder that the Greeks are presently reacting so passionately to the so-called "Macedonian Question". For them, Macedonia is an historically proven Greek-speaking entity invited over two thousand years ago to participate in the Olympic Games when they were closed to all but Greeks. Thus they see any attempt to take the name "Macedonia" and allow it to be used by a territory of the former Yugoslavia as a thinly-disguised pretext for eventually claiming all of Macedonian as other than Greek. It is an age-old problem that will continue to simmer and occasionally come to a dangerous boil for the foreseeable future. Because, depending on how you view this extraordinarily beautiful country, it is as it has always been either a bridge or a stepping stone between Europe and Asia and, as such, highly coveted. As well as colorful.

A VERY BASIC GRAMMAR

The Greek language is Indo-European in origin, and if it seems unique, this is because it is the only member of its subfamily. In prehistoric Greece there were four dialects brought into the area by tribes migrating from central and northern Asia. One of these developed into Attic which, as the dialect of Classical Athens and the language in which its literary and philosophical works were written, inevitably superseded all the others.

During the Hellenistic Age, as Attic became the common language of all the countries conquered by Alexander the Great and ruled over by his successors, it gradually took on characteristics of the people who spoke it and changed into what is now known as "*koine*," i.e. common to all. This language in turn divided into demotic and literary *koine*, the latter being the one in which the Four Gospels were written. Demotic i.e. "popular" *koine* was subsequently further broken down into local dialects. These two versions of Greek survived in their various, mutating forms until the liberation of Greece from Ottoman rule in the 19th century. At this point, Greek scholars and other men of learning created an artificial language called "*katharevousa*," i.e. "clean" or "pure" Greek, which harkened back to Classical Greek and became the official language of the country, the one in which all respectable documents, including literary ones, were supposed to be written. It was taught in schools and used in all government documents and high-minded speeches. However, almost no one spoke it unless absolutely necessary, and with the return of democracy following the fall of the colonels' junta, it was finally abandoned, with the demotic Greek that had been spoken by the people all these centuries at last being given the recognition it deserved. Nevertheless, there are still strong pockets of resistance to this change-over and in even the most up-to-date dictionaries and phrase books you will words or forms of words given that are pure *katharevousa*. Many of these can be recognized by their *-ov* or *-ις* endings.

In order for the examples in the following section to be clearly understood, it is necessary to first explain the phonetic system developed for this book.

PHONETICS

One of the most important aspects of the Greek language is the placing of stress on the correct syllable. Placed on the wrong syllable, it can possibly change the entire meaning of the word, sometimes with disastrous results, as in the following (where **the accented syllable is in bold-face type**);:

line or queue	**oo**ra
urine	oo**ra**

That aside, the pronunciation of Greek is relatively easy for an English-speaking person since all of the vowel and most of the consonant sounds are to be found in English.

As in English, there are two "th" sounds, and these are transliterated phonetically in this book as follows:

    "th" as in "theater": "th" (i.e. **theh**-atro)
    "th" as in "those": "dh" (.i.e. **dheee**ta" - "diet")

The latter is used when the letter δ (capital Δ) is employed, while the former substitutes for the letter θ (capital Θ).

There are some consonant sounds which are virtually impossible to adequately transliterate phonetically. They are as follows:

- **g (γ)**   When followed by an "a" or "o" it is pronounced as in "ghost" but with the "h" clearly aspirated.
- **ps (ψ)**   As in "lips" with the "p" clearly pronounced, even at the beginning of a word.
- **h (η)**   Heavily aspirated, as in "hew" as opposed to "how."

WORD ORDER
With a few exceptions, the basic pattern of Greek phrases and sentences is much the same as in English and can be relatively easy to manage, as the following example will indicate:

Mary drinks coffee with milk and sugar.
Ee Mar**ee**a **pee**nee ka**feh** meh **ga**la kay **za**haree.

The three major exceptions are as follows:
1) Pronouns that are the subjects of sentences are rarely used, as the form of the verb indicates what the subject is: **I want coffee. The**lo ka**feh.**
2) Pronouns that are objects of verbs precede the verb: **I want it.** Toh **the**lo.
3) Possessive pronouns follow the noun they possess: **my coffee** toh ka**feh** mou (lit. "the coffee my").

NOUNS
All nouns have three genders: masculine, feminine, and neuter. Articles and adjectives precede the noun and must conform to its gender. Personal names are also preceded by articles, but only when the person is being spoken about, not when he or she is being spoken to:

Where is Mary?	Poo **ee**nay ee Mar**ee**a?
Hello, Mary!	Ya**soo**, Mar**ee**a!

PERSONAL PRONOUNS
As noted above, since the form of the verb indicates its person, personal pronouns are rarely used as subjects except for emphasis:

Mary's hungry.	Ee Mar**ee**a pee**na**ee.
She's hungry.	Pee**na**ee.
She's hungry again?!	Af**tee** pee**na**ee pah**lee**?!

There are two **verb forms** for "you": one is singular and familiar, being usually used only with friends and close acquaintances; the second is plural (for a number of people) or singular formal (used when speaking to someone you don't know very well or as sign of respect to special or older people).

What do you want?   Tee **thelees**? (singular, familiar)
                        Tee **theleteh**? (plural or formal)

VERBS

These change their forms according to which person (1st, 2nd, 3rd) they are in.

The **negative** is formed by putting "dhen" (i.e "not") before the verb:

Mary isn't hungry.   Ee Mareea dhen peenaee.

The **future tense** is formed by putting "tha" before the infinitive tense of the verb:

She will be hungry.   Tha peenaee.
I will not be hungry.   Dhen tha peenao.

ADVERBS

These follow the verb and are often formed by substituting an "a" ending to an adjective, as we often add "ly":

complete   oloklero
completely   oloklera

INFINITIVES

Often, but not always, formed by adding "na" to the indefinite tense of the verb according to its person:

I want to eat.   Thelo na fao.
She wants to eat.   Thelee na faee.

Certain verbs, however, change their forms when put into the infinitive and future tenses, others do not. Don't worry about it. You will be understood.

DIRECT & INDIRECT OBJECTS

As nouns, these follow the verb:

Peter gave Mary a lamb. Oh **Petros** ehdoseh stee Mareea ena arnee.

As pronouns, they precede the verb:

Peter gave it to her. Oh **Petros** tees (*her*) toh (*it*) ehdooseh.

POSSESSIVES

These follow the object possessed, the object being preceded by its definite article "the":

Peter's lamb	Toh arnee tou **Petrou**
His lamb	Toh arnee tou
Mary's lamb	Toh arnee tees **Mareeas**
Her lamb	Toh arnee tees

But:

It was his, now it's hers. Eetahn dheeko tou, torah eenay dheeko tees.

Finally, most (but not all) nouns have an extra stress added to the last syllable when put into the possessive with a pronoun:

the car	toh afto**kee**nitoh
my car	toh afto**kee**nitoh mou

CONJUNCTIONS

Used exactly as in English:

Mary bought peas and potatoes. Ee Mareea ahgoraseh beezelia kay patatess.

PREPOSITIONS

Certain prepositions, such as "with" (**meh**) and "like" (**sahn**) are used exactly as in English; others, such as "to," "at" and "in" change their form according to the gender and number of their objects. Consequently these are impossible for a beginner to even bother about learning.

PAST TENSES, GERUNDS, GENITIVES, ACCUSATIVE CASES, ETC.
See a real book of Greek grammar, or forget it.

THE GREEK ALPHABET

Greek letter	Greek name of letter
A α	**alfa**
B β	**veeta**
Γ γ	**gah**ma
Δ δ	**dhelta**
E ε	**ep**silon
Z ζ	**zeeta**
H η	**eeta**
Θ θ	**theeta**
I ι	**eeohta**
K κ	**kahpa**
Λ λ	**lahm**dha
M μ	mee
N ν	nee
Ξ ξ	ksee
O o	**oh**meekron
Π π	pee
P ρ	roh
Σ σ, ς	**seeg**ma
T τ	**tahf**
Y υ	**ep**silon
Φ φ	fee
X χ	hee
Ψ ψ	psee
Ω ω	o**meh**ga

GREEK- ENGLISH
ΕΛΛΕΝΙΚΑ – ΑΓΓΛΙΚΑ

A

άβαθος shallow
αβγό egg
αβγολέμονο egg-lemon sauce
άγαλμα statue
άγαμος unmarried *male*
άγαμη unmarried *female*
αγάπη love
αγαπημένος beloved *male*
αγαπημένη beloved *female*
αγαπώ I love
άγγελος angel
αγγλικός *adj.* English
Άγγλος Englishman
Αγγλίδα English woman
αγγούρι cucumber
αγιογραφία icon, holy painting
αγκαλιά embrace, bosom
αγκινάρα artichoke
αγκίστρι fish-hook
άγκυρα anchor
αγορά market
αγόρι boy
άγριος wild
αγροφύλακος rural policeman

άγχος anxiety
αγώνας contest, struggle
αγώνες athletic games
αγονία agony, suspense
άδεια permit, license, "visa," leave of absence
αδειάζω, να to empty
αδελφή sister
αδέλφια brothers, brother(s) and sister(s)
αδελφός brother
αδιαβρόχο raincoat
αδιέξοδο no exit; cul-de-sac
αδύνατος weak; impossible
αέρας air, wind
αεριστήρας fan, ventilator
αεροδρόμιο airport, aeordrome
αερολίμην airport
αεροπλάνο airplane
αεροπορία airline, air force
αεροπορικώς by air
αηδιάστικος disgusting
άθεος atheist
αθλητής athlete
αίθουσα large room, hall
άιντε come on!
αιώνας century, era
ακαδημαικός an academic
ακίνδυνος not dangerous
ακούω hear, listen to, obey
ακριβός expensive
ακριβώς exactly
ακρόπολις upper city, acropolis

ακρωτήριο cape, promontory
ακτή seashore
αλάτι salt
αλεύρι flour
αλήθεια truth; really, truly
αληθιννός genuine, true
αλίμονο alas! oh my goodness!
αλκοολικός an alcoholic
αλλαγή *noun* change
αλλάζω *verb* change
αλλοίος different, not the same
άλλος other, different
άλλη φορά another time;
   κι άλλο some more;
   άλλα δύο two more
 την άλλη φορά next time
αλλού elsewhere
άλογο horse
αλυσίδα chain
αλώνι threshing floor
αμάν for heaven's sake!
αμάξι automobile
αμαρτία sin
αμέ of course!
Αμερικάνικος *adj.* American
Αμερικάνος an American Greek
Αμερικανός an American
αμέσως immediately!
αμήν amen
αμμουδιά sandy beach
άμνος lamb
αμοιβή reward, fee

αμπέλι vineyard
αμύγδαλο almond
αμφθέατρο amphitheater
αμφορεύς amphora
αν if, whether
αναβαίνω go up
αναβάλλω postpone
αναβολή postponement
ανάβω turn on, light
ανάγκκη need, necessity
αναισθητικό anaesthetic
αναλαμβάνω undertake to do
ανάλυση analysis
ανάμικτος mixed
αναπνέω breathe
αναπνοή breath, breathing
ανάποδος wrong way round, backwards
αναπτήρας lighter (cigarette, stove)
ανασκαφή excavation
ανασήλωση restoration (archeological)
ανατολή sunrise; east, Orient
ανδρόγυνο married couple
ανεβάζω carry, lift; raise (prices);
    put on (performance)
ανεμόμυλος windmill
άνεμος wind
ανεξάρτητος independent
ανέξοδος free of charge
άνεση comfort, relaxation;
    με άνεση at leisure
άνετος comfortable, covenient
άνευ without

ανέχομαι tolerate, bear
ανεψιά niece
ανεψιός nephew
άνηθο dill
ανθοδέσμη bouquet of flowers
ανθοδοχείο flower vase
ανθοπώλης florist
άνθος flower
ανθρωπολόγος anthropologist
άνθρωπος man, human being, person
ανίσχυρος not valid; powerless
ανοησία nonsense, foolishness
άνοιγμα opening
ανοίγω *verb* open, turn on
ανοικτός open
αντάμωση:
    καλή αντάμωση au revoir
αντάρτης rebel, guerilla
άντε come on! go!
αντένα aerial
αντί instead of, in return for
αϖτίγραφο copy
αντιγράφω copy
αντίδοτο antidote
αντιδώρον Host
αντιθέτω oppose
αντίκα antique
αντιλυσσικός anti rabies
αντίο goodbye!
αντιπρόεδρος vice-president
αντισηπτικός antiseptic
άντρας man; husband

άνω above, up;
  άνω κάτω upside down, in confusion
ανώτερος superior, senior
αξία value, worth;
αξιές stock market shares
αξιοπρέπια dignity, correctness
απαγορεύω forbid
απαντώ reply
απάνω up, above, on top
απέναντι opposite
απεργία strike, work stoppage
απλός simple, plain
από from, since, of
αποβάθρα railway platform
αποβολή abortion; miscarriage
απόγευμα afternoon
απόδειξη receipt; proof
αποθήκη place for storage
αποκάλυψις revelation; Apocalypse
αποκριές pre-Lent carnival
αποπάνω above; on top
αποσκευές luggage
αποσμητικό deodorant
απόστημα abscess
απόστολος apostle
αποτέλεσμα result; consequence
αποφασίζω *verb* to decide
απόφαση decision
αποφεύγω *verb* to avoid, escape
απόφοιτος *noun* graduate
απόψε tonight
Άραβας Arab

αραβικός Arabian
αράχνη spider
αργά slowly; late
αργότερα later
αριθμός number
αριστερά left; to the left
αρκετά enough, sufficient
αρνί lamb
αρνούμαι *verb* to deny, refuse
αρρώστια illness
άρρωστος ill
αρσενικός male, masculine
αρχαϊκός archaic
αρχή start, beginning
αρχηγός leader
αρχίζω *verb* to begin
άρωμα aroma
ας let's
ασανσέρ elevator
ασήμι silver
ασθενοφόρορον ambulance
ασπιρίνη aspirin
άστακος lobster
αστείο joke
αστέρας star
αστραπή lightning
αστυνομία police
ασφαλεία insurance, security
ασχολία occupation, business
άτακτος unruly
άτομο person
ατυχία bad luck

αυγή dawn
αυθεντικός authentic
αυλή back, side or court yard
αύριο tomorrow
αυτοκίνητο automobile
αφήνω *verb* to let go of, allow
άφιξη arrival
αφίσα poster
αφρός lather, foam, cream
αχινός sea-urchin

B

βαγόνι railway coach; truck
βάζω *verb* to put
βαθμός degree, grade
βάθος depth
βαμβάκι cotton
βαμμένος dyed
βάπτισμα baptism
βαρέλι barrel
βάρκα boat
βασιλεύς king
βασιλκός basil
βασίλισσα queen
βάση base, foundation
βαφή *noun* dye
βγάζω *verb* to take, get, remove
βέβαιως certainly

βεβαιώνω *verb* to confirm, assure
βενζινάκατος motorboat
βεντέττα vendetta, star
βέρα wedding or engagement ring
βεράντα verandah
βήχας *noun* cough
βιάζομαι *verb* be in a hurry
βιασμός *noun* rape
βιβλιοθήκη library
βιβλίο book
βίβλος Bible
βίδα *noun* screw
βίζα visa
βλάκας dumbhead, fool
βλέπω *verb* to see
βολεύω *verb* to fit in; be convenient
βόρειος *adj.* north
βοριάς *noun* north wind
βότανο herb
βουλκανιζατέρ tire repair shop
βούλωμα tire patch; tooth filling
βουνό mountain
βραβείο prize
βράδυ evening
βράζω *verb* to boil
βραστός boiled
βραχιόλι bracelet
βράχος rock
βραχυκύκλωμα short circuit
βρογχίτιδα bronchitis
βροχή rain
βρύση fountain, faucet

βρώμικος dirty
βυζαντινός Byzantine

Γ

γάλα milk
γαλλικός *adj.* French
γάμος wedding
γάντι glove
γάτα cat
γεία health;
   γειά σου! Greetings!
γειτονάς neighbor
γέλιο *noun* laugh, laughter
γεμίζω *verb* to fill, stuff
γεμιστός stuffed
γενεθλιά birthday
γένεια beard
γενικός *adj.* general
γέννηση birth
γεννώ *verb* to give birth
γεράκι hawk
γέρος old man
γερός strong, healthy
γεύμα meal
γεύση *adj.* taste, flavor
γη earth, ground
γιά for
γιαγιά grandmother
γιαλός seashore
γιαούρτι yogurt

γιατί why
γιατί because
γιατρός doctor
γίνομαι *verb* become, happen
γιορτή feast day, name day, holiday
γιός son
γιουβαρλάκια balls of meat and rice
γκάζι paraffin, butane, accelerator
γκαρσόν waiter
γκαρσονιέρα bachelor apartment
γκλίτσα shepherd's crook
γλάρος seagull
γλάστρα flower pot
γλέντι party
γλυκά sweets, pastries
γλύπτης sculptor
γλώσσα tongue
γνήσιος genuine
γνωρίζω *verb* to know, be acquainted with
γνωστός known, recognized
γόμα eraser
γουλιά a sip, mouthful
γούνα *noun* fur
γούστο *noun* good taste
γράμμα *noun* letter (post)
γραμματόσημο postage stamp
γραμμένος written
γραφείο office, bureau, desk
γράφω *verb* to write
γρίππη the flu
γυαλί *noun* glass;
    γιαλια glasses, spectacles

γυμνάσιον secondary school
γυμναστήριον gymnasium
γυμνός naked
γυναίκα woman, wife
γυναικολόγος gynecologist
γυρίζω *verb* to turn
γύφτος male gypsy
γύφτισσα female gypsy

Δ

δανείζω *verb* to lend
δάνειο *noun* loan
δαντέλλα lace
δάσκαλος teacher
δάσος forest, woods
δάφνη laurel
δάχτυλο finger, toe
δαχτυλίδι *noun* finger ring
δεν not
δείγμα sample, specimen
δείπνο supper, dinner
δεκαπενταύγουστος Feast of Assumption, August 15
δελφίνι dolphin
δέμα package, bundle
δέντρο tree
δετρολίβανο rosemary
δένω *verb* to tie up
δεξιά right, to the right
δέρμα skin, leather

δερματινός *adj.* leather
δεσποινίς, δεσποινίδα Miss; young lady
δευτερόλεπτο a second (time)
δέχομαι receive, accept
δηλώνω *verb* to declare, signify
δήμαρχος mayor
δημιουργικός creative
δημοκρατία democracy
δημοσιογράφος journalist
δημόσιος *adj.* public;
   δημόσιος υπάλληλος civil servant
δημοτική the demotic Greek language
διαβάζω *verb* to read
διαβατήριο passport
διάβολος devil
διάδρομος crossroads
διαζύγιο divorce
διακοπή a cutting off; interruption
διακόπτης *noun* switch (elec., etc.)
διαμάντι diamond
διαμέρισμα apartment
διάρροια diarrhea
διαφορά *noun* difference
διαφορετικός different
διαφωνώ *verb* to disagree
διεύθυνσις address
διευθυντής director (not theater)
δικαστήριον law court
δικηγόρος lawyer
δίκιο right; έχω δίκιο I am right.
δίκλινο a double room
δικτατορία dictatorship

δίλημμα dilemma
δίνω *verb* to give
διορθώνω *verb* to correct, fix
διορθωση correction, repair
δίπλα beside, nest to
διπλά twice as much
δίπλωμα diploma
διπλωμάτης diplomat
δίσκος disk (of all sorts)
δίχτυ *noun* net
δίχως without
διψώ *verb* to be thirsty
δόλωμα bait
δόντι tooth
δόξια glory
δόση dose
δουλειά work, job
δουλεύω *verb* to work
δράμα drama
δρόμος road, street
δροσερός cool, fresh
δύναμη strength, power
δυνατός strong, powerful; possible
δυόσμος mint
δύσκολος difficult
δυσπεψία indigestion
δυστύχημα accident, misfortune
δυστυχώς unfortunately
δωμάτιο room
δώρον gift, present

E

εβδομάδα week;
   Μεγαλν Εβδομαδα Holy Week
εβραικός Jewish, Hebrew
Εβραίος a Jewish man
εγγλεζικός English
Εγγλέζο Englishman
εγγύηση guarantee, deposit
έγκλημα crime
έγκυος pregnant
εγώ I; ego
εδώ here
έθιμο custom, tradition
εθνικός national
έθνος nation
είδα I saw.
είδη goods, things to sell
εικόνα image, picture, icon
εικονοκλάστης iconoclast
εικονοστάσι icon hanging wall; shrine
είμαι I am
είναι he is
ειρήνη peace
ειρωνεία irony
εισιτήριο ticket
είσοδος entrance; admission
εισπράκτορας money and ticket collector
εκατομμήριο million
εκατοστάρι 100 drachma note
έκδοση publication, issue. edition
εκδότης publisher

εκδρομή excursion
εκεί there, over there
εκείνος the man over there; that one
έκθεση exhibition
εκθέτω *verb* to exhibit
εκκλησία church
έκπληξη surprise
εκπομπή *noun* broadcast
έκπτωση sale, discount
έκσταση ecstacy
έκτακτος temporary
εκτός outside; except
έκτρωση abortion, miscarriage
έλα come; έλα δω come here!
ελαιόλαδο olive oil
ελαφρός light, mild
Ελβετός Swiss man
ελευθερία freedom
ελεύθερος free; unmarried
ελιά olive, olive tree
έλκος ulcer
Έλλας Greece
Έλληνας a Greek man
Ελληνίδα a Greek woman
ελληνικός *adj.* Greek
ελληνισμός the Greek people; Hellenism
ελπίζω *verb* to hope
εμετός vomiting
εμπόδιο obstacle, hindrance
εμπορικός *adj.* commercial
εμφάνιση appearance

εμπρός forward; hello! (on telephone)
έναρξη beginning
ενδιαφέρων interesting
ένεση injection
ενθύμιο souvenir
εννοώ intend, mean to; understood
ενοικιάζω *verb* to rent
ενοικιαστής tenant
ενοίκιο the rent
ενοχλώ *verb* to annoy, bother
εντελής perfect, complete
έντερο intestine
εξαδελφή female cousin
εξαδελφός male cousin
εξετάση examination
έξοδος exit
εξοχή countryside
έξυπνος clever
έξω outside
εξωτερικός external, foreign
εορτάζω *verb* to celebrate (name day, etc.)
εορτή name day festival; holiday
επάγγελμα profession
επανάσταση revolution
επί τέλους at last!
επιβάτης passenger
επιβαβαιώνω *verb* to confirm
επιταγή bank check, money order
επιτάφιος funeral;
    Good Friday procession
επιτρέπω *verb* to allow
επιτυχία success

Επιφάνια Epiphany
επομένος following, next
εποξή epoch, era
επώνυμο surname
εργάζομαι *verb* to work
εργαλείο tool
εργασία work
εργάτης worker
εργένης bachelor
έρχομαι I am coming.
έρωτας love, passion
ερωτεύομαι I am in love with...
ερώτηση question
ερωτικός erotic
εσύ you
έσω inside
εσώρουξα underwear
εσωτερικός interior, domestic (not foreign)
Ευαγγελισμός Annunciation
ευκαιρία opportunity, bargain
ευκολία convenience
εύκολος easy
ευκόλυνω facilitate
ευροπαικός European
ευχαριστώ Thank you;
 ευχαριστούμαι I am pleased, happy;
 ευχαριστημένος *adj.* pleased, satisfied
εύχομαι I wish, give my blessings
εφημερίδα newspaper
εφιάλτης nightmare
εχθές yesterday
έχω I have.

Z

ζακέτα jacket
ζαλίζω I am dizzy
ζάχαρη sugar
ζαχαροπλαστείο confectionary store
ζεσταίνω *verb* to heat or warm something
ζεσταίνομαι I feel or am getting hot.
ζέστη heat, fever; κάνει ζέστη It (the weather) is hot.
ζεστός *adj.* hot, warm
ζευγάρι couple, pair
ζήτημα question, problem, issue
ζόρι difficulty, trouble
ζουμί broth, juice
ζυγίζω weigh
ζω I live
ζωγραφιά picture
ζωγραφίζω *verb* to paint, draw
ζωγραφός painter, artist
ζωή life, vitality
ζωηρός lively
ζώνη belt, zone
ζωτανός alive, living
ζώον animal

H

ηλεκτρικός electrical

ηλεκτρισμός electricity
ηλίαση sunstroke
ηλικία age
ηλιοθεραπεία sunbathing
ηλιοκαμένος sunburnt
ήλιος sun
ημείς us, we
ημέρα day
ημερόλογιο calendar
ημερομηνία date
ηρέμα calmly
ήρεμος calm, not upset
ήρωας hero
ηρωίδα heroine
ησυχία quietness, peace
ηφαίστειο volcano
ήχος sound

#

θα will (forming future tense)
θάλασσα sea
θαλασσινά shellfish
θάνατος death
θαύμα death
θαυμάσιος wonderful
θεά goddess
θέα view, sight
θέαμα spectacle, show
θεατής spectator
θέατρο theter

θεία aunt
θείος uncle
θέλω I want
θέμα subject, theme, topic
θεός God
Θεοτόκος Mother of God
θεραπεία therapy
θεραπεύω *verb* to treat, cure
θέρμανση heating
θέρμη fever; hot springs
θέσις place, seat, position
θεωρείο theater box
θησαυρός treasure
θρησκεία religion
θύελλα storm
θυμάμαι I remember
θυμάρι thyme
θυμούμαι I remember
θυμώνω I am getting angry *or*
    I make angry.
θυρίδα ticket office, small window

I

Ιάπωνας a Japanese
ιαπωνικός Japanese
ιατρείο doctor's office, clinic
ιατρός doctor
ιδέα idea
ιδιοκτήτης owner
ίδρυμα foundation, institution

ιδρώνω *verb* to sweat
ινστιτούτον institute
ίππος horse
ίσα straight, evenly
ίσιος level, upright, equal to
ισόγειο ground floor
ίσος eaqual to, the same as
ισπανικός Spanish
Ισπανός a Spanish man
ιστιοπλοΐα sailing
ιστορία history; story
ιστορικός historical, historic
ίσως perhaps
ιταλικός Italian
Ιταλός an Italian man

Κ

κάβα wine cellar
καβγάς quarrel, argument
καβούρι crab
καζανάκι toilet, cistern
καημένος burnt; unfortunate, poor
καθαρίζω *verb* to clean
καθάρισμα cleaning
καθαρίστρια cleaning woman
καθαρός clean
κάθε each, every
καθήζω *verb* to sit
καθολικός catholic
καθόλου not at all, none at all

κάθομαι I am seated
καθρέπτης mirror
καθυστέρηση delay
και and, also, even
καΐκι caique
καινούργιος new
καιρός time, period, weather
καίω *verb* to be burning; to burn.
κακά badly
κακάο cocoa
κακός bad, evil, harmful;
  κακό μάτη evil eye
καλά *adverb* well, properly, okay.
καλαμάκι drinking straw; small wooden skewer
κάλαντα Christmas and New Year carols
καλημέρα Good morning!
καληνύξτα Good night
καλησπέρα Good evening.
καλλιτέχνης artist
καλόγερος monk
καλός good
καμάκι trident;
  καμάκης man who tries to pick up girls
κανέλλα cinnamon
κανένας no one
κάνω *verb* to do, make
καπέλλο cap, hat
κάπνισμα smoking
καπνιστός smoked
καπνός smoke
κάποτε sometimes; once
κάπου somewhere

καράφα carafe
κάρβουνο charcoal
καρδιά heart
καρκίνος cancer
καρναβάλι carnival
καρροτζάκι pushcart
κάρτα postcard; card
καρφί nail
καρφίτζα pin, brooch
καρφώνω *verb* to nail
κάστρο castle, fortress
καταβολή payment
κατάρα *noun* curse
καταρράκτης cataract
κατασκευάζω construct, manufacture
κατάστημα shop, office
κατάστρωμα deck of a ship
κατά τύχη by chance
κατεβάζω *verb* to bring down; descend
κατεβαίνω *verb* to come or go down
κάτι some, certain, something
κατσαβίδι screwdriver
κατσίκι kid, goat
κάτω below
καυτερός hot, peppery
καφενείο coffee shop
καφές coffee
καφεζής cafe owner or manager
κέντημα embroidery, needlework
κέντρο center
κεραμική ceramics
κεράσι cherry

κερατάς cuckold
κερδίζω *verb* to earn, win
κέρδος profit
κερί wax; candle
κεφάλι head
κέφι extreme, god-given happiness
κηδεία fineral
κήπος garden
κιβώτιο large box, trunk
κιμάς ground meat
κινέζικα Chinese; sth. unintelligible
κίνηση traffic; movement
κιόσκι kiosk
κλέβω *verb* to steal, rob
κλειδαριά *noun* lock
κλειδί key
κλειδώνω *verb* to lock.
κλείνω *verb* to close
κλειστός closed
κλέφτης thief
κληρονόμος heir
κλίμα climate
κλιματισμός air-conditioning
κλινική clinic
κλύσμα enema
κλωστή thread
κόβω *verb* to cut
κοιλιά belly
κοιμούμαι *verb* to sleep, go to bed.
κοιτάζω *verb* to look at, look after
κόκκαλο bone
κόκκινος red, red-faced

κοκορέτσι grilled sheep's entrails
κόλαση hell
κόλλα glue
κόλλυβα a boiled wheat dish, sweet, served at memorial service
κολόνια cologne
κόλπος gulf, bay
κολύμπι swimming
κόμβος knot
κόμμα political party
κομμάτι a piece, bit
κομμένος cut up, ground
κομμωτέριο hairdresser's
κομπόστα stewed fruit
κοντά near
κοντεύω I am almost done, near.
κοπέλλα young woman, girl
κοπή cutting
κοπριά manure
κορδέλλα ribbon, tape
κορδόνι cord, shoe lace
κόρη daughter, girl
κορίτσι girl
κόσμος world, people
κοστίζω cost
κουβέντα discussion, talk
κουβέρτα blanket
κούκλα doll
κουκουβάγια owl
κουκουνάρι pine cone, pine nut
κουλούρι donut-twisted biscuit, bread
κουμπί button

κουνέλι rabbit
κουνουπιέρα mosquito-net
κουπί oar
κούραση fatigue
κουραστικός tired
κουρείο barbershop
κουτί box
κουφέτο sugar-covered almond
κουφός deaf
κράνος helmet
κρασί wine
κράτος state (political entity)
κρατώ keep, have, hold
κρέας meat
κρεβάτι bed
κρεμώ *verb* to hang
κρίμα sin; a pity
κρίση crisis
κρύβω *verb* to hide
κρυμμένος hidden
κρύο *noun* cold
κρυολόγημα a headcold etc.
κρύος *adj.* cold
κρυφά secretly
κρυώνω I am cold, I am getting cold.
κτήμα property, land
κτηνίατρος veterinary
κυβέρνησις government
κυδώνι quince
κύκλος circle
κυκλοφορώ *verb* to circulate
κυκλοφορία circulation

κύκλωμα electric circuit
κύμα *noun* wave
κυνηγώ *verb* to hunt
κύπελλο cup
κυρία lady, madam, Mrs.
κύριος lord, mister, Mr.
κώλος bottom, ass
κωμωδία comedy

Λ

λαγός hare
λαδερός oily
λάδι oil
λαδολέμονο oil-lemon dressing
λάθος mistake
λαιμός throat
λάμα blade
λάμπα bulb, light
λαμπρός brilliant, bright
λαός people, race, the common people
λαούτο lute
λάσπη mud
λάστιχο rubber band, elastic
λατρεύω *verb* to adore, worship
λαχείο lottery
λεβέντης admirable young man
λέγω, λέω *verb* to say
λείπω *verb* to miss, be away;
    μου λείπει I miss it.
λειτουργώ *verb* to function, work

λεκάνη basin, bowl, pelvis
λεκές spots
λεξικό dictionary
λεπτά money
λεπτομέρεια details
λεπτό minute (time)
λεπτός thin, slim
λερωμένος dirty
λευκός white
λεωφορείο bus
λεωφόρος avenue
λιγάκι a little
λίγο a little
λιμάνι port, harbor
λίπος fat
λιμενάρχης harbor master
λογαριασμός the bill, check
λόγια words
λογικός logical
λόγος word, speech; reason
λοιπόν well! so! listen!
λόρδος Lord
λουκάνικο sausage, hot dog
λουκέτο padlock
λουκούμι Turkish delight
λουλούδι flower
λουξ deluxe
λουρί strap, belt
λουτρό bath
λυπάμαι *verb* to be sorry for
λύπη regret, pity
λυπημένος sad, sorry

λυπούμαι I am sorry.
λύση solution, answer
λύσσα rabies

M

μα but
μαγαζί store, shot
μαγεία magic, sorcery
μαγειρεύω *verb* to cook
μαγειρίτσα Easter soup
μάγισσα witch, sorceress
μαγνητιφώνο tape recorder
μαέστρος music conductor
μαζεύω *verb* to gather together
μαζί together
μαθαίνω *verb* to learn
μάθημα lesson
μαθητής pupil
μαιμού monkey
μακάρι! I should hope so!
μακριά far
μακρύς long, tall
μαλάκας masturbator, jerk
μαλακός soft, mild
μαλλί wool; hair
μαλλιά hair (head)
μαμμή midwife
μανάβης greengrocer
μανία madness, passion, mania
μάννα mother

μαντήλι kerchief; handkerchief
μαντινάδα Cretan song
μάππας idiot
μαραγκός carpenter
μάραθο fennel
μαργαριτάρι pearl
μαρίδα whitebait
μάρτυς witness; martyr
μάτι eye; κακό μάτι evil eye; ματιά μου my darling!
ματιάζω *verb* to give s.o. the evil eye
μαυρίζω *verb* to darken; become tanned
μαυροδάφνη a sweet red wine
μαύρος *adj.* black
μαχαίρι knife
μάχη battle
με with
μεγάλος large, big
μέγεθος size
μεζές appetizers
μεθυσμένος *adj.* drunk
μείον less, minus
μέλισσα bee
μέλλων future
μένω *verb* to stay, remain; reside at (in)
μέρα day
μερίδα portion, helping
μεροκκάματο daily wage
μέρος place; toilet
μέσα inside; τα μέσα money
μεσάνυχτα midnight
μέση middle; waist

μεσημέρι noon
μεσίτης broker, real estate agent
μεσόγειος Mediterranean
μέσον middle way, means; inside influence
μετά afterwards; after
μετακομίζω *verb* to move house
μέταξα silk
μεταφέρω *verb* to carry, transport
μεταφορά transportation, conveyance
μεταφοράζω *verb* to transport
μέτριος medium; medium-sweet coffee
μετρώ *verb* to measure, count
μέχρι until
μη don't
μηδέν zero
μήνας month
μήνυμα message
μητέρα mother
μήτρα womb, uterus
μητροπολίτης metropolitan bishop
μηχανή machine, engine
μηχανικός *noun* mechanic, engineer
μία one, a, an
μικρός small, little
μικτός mixed
μιλώ *verb* to speak
μινωικός Minoan
μισό *noun* half
μίσος hatred
μισύ *adj.* half
μισώ *verb* to hate

μνημείο monument
μνήμη memory; a remembrance
μόδα fashion
μοιάζω *verb* to resemble
μοίρα fate
μοιράζω *verb* to apportion;
  share out
μοιχεία adultery
μόλις just as, just now
μοναδικός unique. sole
μοναξιά solitude, loneliness
μοναστήρι monastery
μονάχος only, alone
μονή monastery
μόνιμος permanent
μονογραφή initials
μονόκλινο single-bed room
μόνο only
μονοπάτι path
μόνος alone, only
μορφή form, face, aspect
μοσχάρι veal
μούντζα insulting open palm gesture
μούσα muse; μούσες muses
μουσείο museum
μουσουλμάνος Muslim
μούτρο face
μούχλα mould
μπάγκος bench, counter
μπαίνω *verb* to enter, go in
μπακάλης grocer
μπάλωμα *noun* patch

μπαμπάκι cotton
μπαμπάς papa
μπάνιο bath
μπεκρής drunkard
μπερδεύω confuse, entangle
μπογιά paint, dye
μπόρα squall
μπορώ *verb* can, be able to
μπουγάτσα cream-filled pastry
μπουζί spark plug
μπουνάτσα calm weather (at sea)
μπρίκι Greek coffee-making pot
μυαλό brain
μύγα fly (insect)
μυθιστόρημα novel
μυθολόγια mythology
μυρίζω *verb* to smell;
  to have an odor
μυρωδιά odor
μυστικό *noun* secret
μωρό baby

N

ναός temple, church
ναργιλές hookah
νεκρός dead
νέος young, new
νερό water
νευρικός nervous
νεφέλη cloud

νέφος smog
νησί island
νηστεία fasting, usu. for Lent
νίκη victory
νιπτήρας wash basin
νοικοκυρά housewife; landlady
νοικοκύρης man of the house
νομάρχης mayor
νόμος law
νονά godmother
νονός godfather
νόστιμος tasty
νότιος south, southern
νούμερο number (telephone)
νταντέλα lace
ντολμάς stuffed vine or cabbage leaf
ντουλάπι cupboard
ντους shower
ντροπαλός shy
ντροπή shyness, shame
νυστάζω *verb* to be sleepy
νύφη bride
νύχι finger or toe nail
νύχτα night

Ξ

ξανά again
ξανθός blond-haired
ξεναγός tourist guide or guidebook
ξενοδοχείον hotel

ξένος foreigner, stranger
ξερός dried
ξέρω *verb* to know
ξεχνώ *verb* to forget
εηρός dried ;
   ξεροί καρποί dried fruits, nuts
ξινός sour, acid
ξύδι vinegar
ξύλο wood
ξυπνητήρι alarm clock
ξυπνώ *verb* to awake
ξύρισμα *noun* shave, shaving

Ο

οδηγός guide, driver
οδηγώ *verb* to guide, drive
οδοντίατρος dentist
οδοντόβουρτσα toothbrush
οδοντογλυφίδα toothpick
οδοντόπαστα toothpaste
οδυσσεία odyssey
οικία house
οικογένεια family
οικοκύρης landlord, householder
οικόπεδο building plot
οίκος house
οινόπνευμα alcohol
ολόκληρος whole, entire
όλος all, everybody, everything
Ολύμπια Olympic games;

Ολυμπιακός Olympic
ομάδα team
ομιλία speech, homily
όμορφος beautiful
ομοφυλοφιλία homosexuality
όνειρο dream
όνομα name
όπισθεν behind, reverse
όποιος whoever
όποτε whenever
όπως as, like
οργάνωσης organization
οργία orgies
ορεκτικά appetizers
όρεξη appetite
όρθιος upright, standing
ορθόδοξος orthodox;
   ορθοδοξία Orthodoxy
όρος mountain;
   Άγιον Όρος Mt. Athos
όσιος blessed, holy
όταν when
ούρα urine
ουρά tail, line (queue)
ούτε not even
όχημα vehicle
όχι no
οχιά viper

Π

πάγκος bench

παγώνω *verb* to freeze
παγωτό ice cream
πάθος passion; illness
παιγνίδι game, toy
παιδάκι little child
παιδεία education, learning
παιδί child; παιδιά children
παίζω *verb* to play
παίρνω *verb* to get, receive, hold
πάλι again
παληκάρι a brave young man, upstanding, admirable
παλτό overcoat
πανί cloth, sail, baby's napkin
πάντα always
παντελόνι pants, trousers
παντοκράτωρ Almighty Lord
παντού everywhere
παντρεμένος married
παντρεύω *verb* to marry
παπαδιά wife of a priest
παπαρούνα poppy
παπάς priest
παπούτσι slippers
παππούς grandfather
παραλία seashore, sea-front
παραμύθι fairy tale
παράνομος illegal
παραπάνω up above
παράσταση theatrical performance
παρέα group of friends
παρέλαση parade

παρθένα virgin
πάρκο park
πασατέμπο sth. to pass time; pumpkin seeds
παστουρμάς very pungent cured meat
Πάσχα Easter
πατήρ father
πατριάρχης patriarch
πατρώνυμο surname
πατσάς tripe soup
πάτωμα floor
παχαίνω *verb* to become fat, overweight
πάω *verb* to go
παθαίνω *verb* to die
πεθερά mother-in-law
πεθερός father-in-law
πειρασμός temptation
πέλαγος open sea
πελάτης customer
πένθος mourning, grief
πέος penis
πέρασμα crossing, passage
περήφανος proud
περιβόλι garden, orchard
περιουσία property, estate
περιοχή region, area, district
περίπατος *noun* a walk, ride, drive around
περιπέτεια adventure
περίπτωση circumstance
περιστέρι pigeon, dove
πέτρα stone
πέφτω *verb* to fall, drop

πηγάδι well (for water)
πηγαίνω *verb* to go to, take to
πηγή spring, source
πηρούνι fork
πήττα flat circular bread; cake; pie
πιά any longer, at last
πιάνω *verb* to catch hold of
πίεση pressure
πιθανός probable, likely
πικρός bitter, sour
πινακίδα license plate
πινέλο artist's paint brush
πίνω *verb* to drink
πιοτό a drink
πισίνα swimming pool
πισινός back, rear, backside
πιστεύω *verb* to believe
πίστις faith, trust
πίσω behind, back
πλάι at the side, next door
πλάκα plaque, paving stone;
    έχει πλάκα It's a joke.
πλάτανος plane tree
πλατεία town square
πλευρό side; rib
πληγή wound, sore
πληρώνω *verb* to pay
πληρωμένος *adj.* paid for
πλοίο ship
πλούσιος weathy
πλυντήριο washing machine
πνεύμα spirit

πνίγω *verb* to drown, choke
ποδήλατο bicycle
πόδι foot
ποδόσφαιρο football
ποίημα poem
ποίηση poetry
ποιητής poet
ποικιλία variety, selection of
ποιότης quality
πόλεμος war
πόλις city, town
πολίτης citizen
πολύ a lot, very much
πονηρός cunning, foxy
πονόλαιμος sore throat
πόνος pain
πόντος centimeter
πόρνη whore
πόρτα door
πορτοκάλι orange
ποτοφόλι wallet
πόσιμος fit for drinking
πόσο how much
ποτάμι river
πότε when
ποτέ never
ποτήρι glass
ποτό drink, beverage
πού where
πουθενά nowhere
πουκάμισο shirt
πουλάκι little bird

πούλμαν chartered bus
πούστης slang homosexual, fairy
πουτάνα whore
πράγμα thing
πράκτωρ agent
πρακτορείο agency
πράσινος green
πρέπει must, have to
πρίζα electric socket
πριν before, ago
προ before, in front of
πρόβα rehearsal
πρόβατο sheep
πρόβλημα problem
πρόγραμμα program, plan, intinerary
προγραμματίζω *verb* to plan, organize
πρόεδρος president
προηγούμενος preceding, previous
προκαταβολή down payment
προλαβαίνω *verb* to anticipate; arrive in time
προξενείο embassy
προ–πό football pools
προς to, towards
προσαρμόζω *verb* to fit, adapt to
προσευχή prayer
προσέχω *verb* to pay attention to, be careful
πρόσκληση invitation
προσπάθεια *noun* try, attempt
προσπαθώ *verb* to try, attempt
προσφορά *noun* offer
προσωπικός *adj.* personal

πρόσωπο face
προτιμώ *verb* to prefer
προχθές the day before yesterday
πρωθυπουργός prime minister
πρωινό breakfast
Πρωτομαγιά May Day
πρώτος first
Πρωτοχρονιά New Year's Day
πτήσις flight (airplane)
πύλη gate (of city, palace, etc.)
πύον pus
πυρετός fever
πώμα cork, stopper
πως how?; why not?

Ρ

ράβω *verb* to sew
ραδιόφωνο radio
ράφτης tailor
ρεβεγιόν Christmas or New Year's Eve party
ρεμπέτικο popular songs of immigrants
ρετσίνα resin-flavored wine
ρίγανη oregano
ρίχνω *verb* to throw, pour, sprinkle
ρόδα wheel
ρολόι clock, watch
Ρούμελη area of Central Greece
ρωμαίικος of modern Greece
    (as opposed to classical)
ρωτώ *verb* to ask

Σ

σακκούλα sack, bag (paper, plastic, etc.)
σαπούνι soap
σαρακοστή Lent
σαύρα lizard
σεις you
σένα you
σεντόνι sheet
σερβίτσιο place setting, service
σηκώνω *verb* to raise, carry
σημαία flag
σημασία meaning, importance
σιγά slowly
σίγουροα for sure, certain
σίδερο iron
σιδερώνω *verb* to iron
σιδηρόδρομος railway
σκάλα stairs, steps
σκάρα grill, grate, rack
σκέπη cover, protection
σκέψη thought
σκηνή stage, scene
σκηνοθεσία stage direction
σκήτη small dependent monastery
σκίσιμο tear, rent
σκληρός hard, difficult
σκάνη dust, powder
σκόρδο garlic
σκοτάδι dark, darkness

σκοτώνω *verb* to kill
σκοτώνομαι *verb* to hurt oneself
σκουλαρίκι earring
σκούπα broom
σκουριά rust
σκύλος dog
σοβαρός serious
σόμπα room-heating stove
σούβλα pit, skewer
σπάζω *verb* to break, smash
σπάνιος rare
σπίτι house
σταθερός stable, steady
σταθμός station
στάσις stop (bus, etc.)
σταυροδρόμι crossroads
σταυρός cross
σταφίδες raisins
σταφύλι grapes
στεγνός dry
στενός narrow
στέρνα cistern
στεφάνι wreath
στιγμή moment
στοιχίζω *verb* to cost; cause pain, grief
στόμα mouth
στραγάλια roasted chickpeas
στρατιώτης soldier
στρατός army
στρίβω *verb* to turn, twist
στρόγγυλος round, circular
στροφή turn

στρώμα mattress
στρώνω το κρεβάτι *verb* to make the bed
στυλό pen
συγγραφεύς writer
σύζυγος spouse
σύκο fig
συλλυπητύρια condolences
συπαθητικός sympathetic; likable
συμπληρώνω complete, fill in
συμφωνία agreement
συμφωνώ *verb* to agree
συν plus
συνάλλαγμα foreign currency
συναυλία concert
συνεχίζω *verb* to continue
συνθέτης composer
σύννεφο cloud
σύνολο sum, total
συνταγή recipe, prescription
σύνταγμα constitution
σύντομα quickly
σφάλμα fault, error
σφίγγω *verb* to squeeze, tighten
σφιχτός tight
σφουγγάρι sponge
σφραγίζω *verb* to stamp or seal
σφύρα hammer
σχεδιάζω *verb* to draw, sketch, plan
σχέδιο sketch, plan, design
σχεδόν almost, nearly
σχέση relation, connection, love affair
σχολείο school

σώζω *verb* to save, rescue
σωλήνας pipe, tube
σώμα body
σωσίβιο life-jacket
σωστός correct, right, real
σωφροσύνη sense, moderation

T

ταβάνι ceiling
τάβλι backgammon
τάδε such-and-such
τάληρο five-drachma piece
ταμπέλα license plate
ταμπλό picture
ταξιδεύω *verb* to travel
τάπα cork, stopper
τάπης carpet, rug
τασάκι ashtray
ταύρος bull
τάφος grave, tomb
ταχεία express train
ταχυδρομείο post office
ταχυδρόμος postman
ταψί baking tin
τείχος wall
τέλειος perfect, complete
τελειώνω *verb* to finish, use up
τελετή ceremony, rite
τέλος end
τελωνείον customs

τέρας monster, freak
τέρμα end, terminus
τέταρτο quarter (of an hour)
τετράγωνο square, city block
τετράδιο notebook
τέχνη craft, art
τζάμι window pane
τζαμί mosque
τζάμπα for nothing, free
τζατζίκι yogurt, cumcumber and garlic mix
τηγανητός fried
τηγάνι frying pan
τηλεγράφημα telegram
τηλεόραση television
τηλέφωνο telephone
τι what?
τίλιο lime flower tea
τιμή price
τίμιος honest
τιμόνι steering wheel; rudder
τίποτα nothing; don't mention it!
τίτλος title
τμήμα police station
τοιούτος homosexual
τοιχίζω *verb* to enclose with a wall
τοίχος wall
τόκος interest (financial)
τοξικός toxic, poisonous
τόπος place, site, ground
τόσο so much
τότε then, in that case
τουαλέτα toilet

τούμπα mound
τουρίστας tourist
Τούρκος Turk
τουρσί sth. pickled
τούρτα cake
τούτος this one
τραβώ *verb* to pull, drag
τράγος goat
τραγούδι song
τραγουδιστής singer
τραγωδία tragedy
τραίνο train
τράπεζα bank
τραπέζι table
τράπουλα deck of cards
τραύμα wound, injury
τρέλλα madness
τρελλός crazy, mad
τρέχω *verb* to run, hurry
τρίβω *verb* rub, grate
τρίκυκλο tricycle (often motorized)
τρίποδο tripod, easel
τρίχα hair
τρίχες hairs; nonsense, lies
τρομάζω *verb* to frighten
τρόμος fright
τρόφιμα food
τροχαία traffic police
τρύπα hole
τρώγω *verb* to eat
τσάι tea
τσάντα handbag, shopping bag

τσατσάρα comb
τσέπη pocket
τσιγάρο cigarette
τσιγγάνος gypsy
τσιμέντο cement
τσιμπώ *verb* to pinch, prick
τσίρκο circus
τυρί cheese
τυχερός lucky
τύχη luck
τώρα now

Υ

υγεία health
υγρός *noun* liquid
υλικός material
υπάλληλος employee, official, clerk
υπέρταση high blood pressure
ύπνος sleep
υπνωτικό sleeping pill
υπόγειο basment
υπογραφή signature
υπολογίζω estimate
υπομονή patience
υπόταση low blood pressure
υποχρέωση obligation
υποψία suspicion
ύστερα later
ύψος height

Φ

φάβα yellow pea puree
φαγητό food
φαΐ food to eat
φανάρι lantern, flashlight, headlight
φανερός clear, obvious
φαντάζομαι *verb* to imagine, suppose
φαράγγι gorge, ravine
φάρδος width
φαρμάκι poison
φάρμακο medicine
φάρος lighthouse
φεγγάρι moon
φελλός cork
φέρω *verb* to bring, carry
φεύγω *verb* to leave, depart
φήμη fame
φιάλη bottle
φιγούρα figure
φίδι snake
φιλί kiss
φιλιά kisses
φιλία friendship
φιλοξενία hospitality
φιλότιμο personal pride, dignity
φιλώ *verb* to kiss
φλιτζάνι cup
φλόγα flame
φλοκάτη thick rug, blanket
φοιτώ *verb* to be a student

φοιτητής male student
φοιτήτρια female student
φόντο bottom, background
φορά way, time;
    άλλη φορά another time
φορείον stretcher
φόρμα form, mold, shape
φόρος tax, duty
φορτηγό truck, freighter
φορτίζω *verb* to charge a battery
φορτίο cargo, load
φορώ *verb* to wear
φουρνάρης baker
φούρνος oven, bakery
φούσκα balloon, blister
φουσκώνω *verb* to inflate, swell
φούστα skirt
φρένο brake
φρέσκος fresh
φρίκη frightful
φροντίζω *verb* to take care of, look after
φροντιστήριο tutoring school
φτηνός cheap
φυλακή jail
φυσικός natural
φυτεύω *verb* to plant
φώκια seal (animal)
φωνή voice; shout
φως light
φωτιά fire
φωτογραφία photograph
φωτογραφική μηχανή camera

Χ

χάζι pleasure, amusment
χαζός stupid
χαίρω *verb* to be glad
χαλί carpet, rug
χαλκιάς coppersmith
χαλκός copper
χαμένος lost, good-for-nothing
χαμηλός low
χαμομήλι chamomile
χάνω *verb* to lose, miss
χάος chaos
χαρά joy, pleasure
χαρακτήρας character
χάρτης paper; map
χαρτί paper
χαρτόσημο official stamp
χασάπης butcher
χείλι lip
χειμόνας winter
χειροτεχνία handicraft
χέρι hand
χήρος widower
χθές yesterday
χιόνι snow
χονδρός thick
χορεύω *verb* to dance
χορός a dance; choir, chorus
χόρτα green vegetables, dandelion greens, etc.

χρειάζομαι *verb* to need, be necessary
χρήματα money
χρησιμοποιώ *verb* to use
Χριστός Christ
χρονιά years
χρόνος time
χρυσός gold
χρώμα color
χρωστώ *verb* to owe
χτίζω *verb* to build
χτίριο building
χτυπώ *verb* to knock, beat, clap
χύμα loose; not packaged or bottled
χώμα earth, soil
χώνευση digestion
χώρα chief town or village; country, land
χωράφι field
χωριάτης someone from a village; peasant
χωριατικός *adj.* peasant
χωρίζω *verb* to divide, divorce, separate
χωριό village
χωρίς without
χωρισμένος divided, divorced
χωριστά separately
χωροφύλακας policeman
χωράω *verb* to fit or have space for

ψάθα straw; straw hat; rush mat
ψαλίδι scissors

ψαράς fisherman
ψαρεύω *verb* to fish
ψάρι fish
ψάχνω *verb* to search for
ψέμα lie, falsehood
ψεύδομαι *verb* to lie
ψεύτης a liar
ψευτικός false, artificial
ψηλός tall, high
ψημένος cooked, roasted
ψήνω *verb* to cook, roast, bake
ψητό roast or grilled meat
ψηφίζω *verb* to vote
ψιλά small change, money
ψιλός thin, fine
ψύλλος flea
ψυχή soul, spirit
ψωμάς baker
ψωμί bread
ψωνίζω *verb* to shop

Ω

ωμός raw
ώρα hour, time
ωραία beautifully, good
ωραίος beautiful
ώροιμος ripe, mature
ωρολόγιο clock, watch

ENGLISH-GREEK
ΑΓΓΛΙΚΑ–ΕΛΛΕΝΙΚΑ

A

a, an *masculine:* **en**as;
feminine: **mee**a; *neuter:* **en**a
abbess eegoumeni
abbot eegoumenos
ability (*competence*) eekanotees
able: I am able. Boroh.
   Is she/he able? Boree?
abortion ektrosee
about (*approximately*) peh-reepoo
above epahno
abroad sto eksoteriko
academic (*adj.*) ahka-dheemah-eekos
academy ahka-dheemeea
accelerator gahzee
accent *stress, mark* **toh**nos;
pronunciation proforah
accident dheesteekheema
accommodation katalima
according to kata seemfona meh
acquaintance (*male*) gnostos; (*female*) gnostee ; **Pleased to make your**
   acquaintance. Hayro polee.
Acropolis Ahkropolees
actor eethopeeos
actress eethopee-ee

adapter prosarmostees
addition prosthesi; **is wrong** eenay lathos;
 in addition to epee-plehon
address dhee-eftheensi
adultery meeheea
adventure peripetia
Aegean Ay-yay-on
Aegina Ay-yeena
Aeschylus Oh Ays-heelos
affair *love* erotihee sk hessee
afford: I can't afford. Dhen ehho ta mehsa.
afraid: I am afraid of... Fo vahmeh...
after metah; **the day after** ee mehra mehtah
afternoon ahpoyevma;
 this afternoon aftoh toh ahpoyevma;
 tomorrow afternoon ahvrio toh ahpoyevma
 good afternoon! Hayreteh!
Again pahlee *or* ksana
Agamemnon Oh Agamemnon
age (*noun*) epohee
agency praktoreeo;
 travel agency praktoreeo taksidheeon
agent praktor
ago preen; **an hour ago** Preen meea ora
agree: I agree Seemfono;
 Do you agree? Seemfonees?
agreement seemfoneea
aid voeethia; **first aid** protess voeethiess
AIDS ayds
ailment ahrostia
air ah-ehras; **fresh air** katharos ah-ehras
air conditioner meehanee kleematismoo
air-conditioning kleematismos
airline ah-eroporikee gramee

GREEK DICTIONARY AND PHRASEBOOK

air mail (by) ah-eroporikos
airplane ah-eroplahno
airport ah-erodhromio
alabaster ahlavastros
alarm clock kseepniteeree
alcohol eenopnevma
alcoholic (*male*) alko-olikos
alcoholism alko-olimos
Alien's Bureau ee Epireseea Allo-dhapon
alive (*male*) zodanos;
   (*female*) zodanee; (*neuter*) zodano
all (*male*) ohlos;
   (*female*) ohlee; (*neuter*) ohlo
allergy ahler-yeea
allowed: Is it allowed? Epitreh-peteh?
Almonds ahmeeg-dhala
almost skheh-dhon
alone (*male*) mohnos;
   (*female*) mohnee; (*neuter*) mohno;
   Leave me alone! Ahseh meh!
alphabet alfaveetoh
also epeesees
alter: to alter na metatrepsees
always pahndoteh
a.m. pro mesimvreeas (Π.M. *or* π.μ.)
ambassador presveftees
amber kek-rimbahree
ambulance ahsthenoforos
America Ahmeriikee
American (*male*) Ahmerikanos;
   (*female*) Ahmerikaneedha
amount pohso
amphitheater amfeetheh-atro
amphora amfor-reh-as

amusement park Luna Park
analysis ahnaleesi
ancestor progonos
anchor ahnkeera
ancient arhayo;
 the ancient Greeks ee arhayee Eliness
and kay; **and that** kay aftoh
anemia ahnaymeea
anesthetic ahnays-thitiko
angry (*male*) theemomenos;
 (*female*) theemomenee
animal zo-oh; **animals** zo-ah
ankle astragalos
annoyed: I am annoyed M'enokleeteh
another ahlo *or* ahkoma;
 another one ahlo (ahkoma) ena
answer (*reply*) ahpahndisi; (*solution*) leesi
ant mirmeeg-hee
antenna keraya
antibiotic ahn-tivee-otikos
antique (*adj.*) arhayo
antique (*noun*) anteeka
antiquities arhay-oh-titess
antiseptic ahntiseeptikos
anxiety ahniseeheea
anxious (*male*) ahn-ee-si-hos;
 (*female*) ahn-ee-si-hee
anyone kahnenahs *or* kahnees
anywhere poothenah
apartment dhee-ahmeh-risma
apartment building pohlikatiheea
apiece toh ena ; **How much apiece?**
 Pohso kosteesi toh ena?
Apollo Oh Ahpohlon

apologize: I apologize Seegnomee
   or Meh See-horr**ees**.
apology ahpolo-y**ee**a
apparently kathos faynetay
appendicitis skolee-ho-eedh**ee**tees
appetite:
   Good appetite! Kahlee or-reksi!
appetizers mezeh *or* mezehdhakia
apple meelo
appliances: electrical appliances
   eelektrik**ess** seeskev**ess**
appointment rahndehvoo
appraiser ekteem**ee**tees
approximately pehreepoo
April Ahpreelios
Arab (*male*) **Ah**ravahs
arcade (shopping) stoah
archbishop arhee-epeeskopos
archeological arhayologhikos
   archeological site arhayologhikee
archeologist arhayologos
architect arheetekton
architecture arheetektonikee
area periohee
area code toh ahftoh-matoh
Aristophanes Oh Ahreestofahnees
Aristotle Oh Ahreestotelees
arm hehree
army, the oh strahtohs;
   army (*adj.*) strahtiotikoh
arrange, to na kahnoneeso
arrest: under arrest eepo kratiseen
arrival ahfeeksi
arrive na fthano;

I will arrive Tha fthaso;
He/she/it will arrive Tha fthasi;
When does it arrive? Poteh tha fthasi?
Art tekhnee; **work of art** ehrgo tekhnee
art gallery pinakotheekee
art supplies eedhee zografikees
artist kaliteknees; **artistic** kalitekneeko
artificial pseftiko
as soon as possible
 ohso toh dhinaton grigorotera
ashamed: I'm ashamed Dhrepomay
ashtray tasahki
ask na'roteeso;
 Will you ask? Tha'roteesees?
asleep keemateh;
 I was asleep. Keemomoona.
aspirin ahspireenee;
 for children dheeah paydiah
assistant voeethos
asthmatic asthmatikos
at the hotel sto ksenodhoheeo
at home sto speetee
at least too lah-heeston
at once ahmessos
Athens Ee Ahtheena
athlete ahthleetees
athletics ahthleeteesmos
Attention! Prosokhee!
 Pay attention (*careful*). Prosekheh.
August Ahvgoustos
aunt theeah
au revoir kahlee ahndamosi
Australia Ahvstraleeah
Australian (*male*) Ahvstralos

Australian (*female*) Ahvstralehza
authentic ahfthentikos
author singrafayahs
automatic ahftohmatoh
automobile ahftokeenitoh
autumn ftheenoporo
avenue leh-oforos
awake:awake me at nine o'clock.
  Kseepnameh stees enaya ee ora.
away *far* makriah;
  He/she is away. Leepee *or* Efeegeh.

B

baby moroh *or* behbees
  baby bottle beebehron;
  baby food paydhikess trofess;
  baby oil paydhiko lahdhee;
  baby powder paydhikee poudhra;
  baby sitter baybee seetehr
Bacchus Oh Bahkhos
bachelor ahgamos *or* ergyeness
back (*adverb*) peeso
back (*noun*) plahtee
backache: I have a backache.
  Ponaee ee plahtee mou.
backgammon tahvlee
backpack sakeedhio
bad (*male*) kakos, (*female*) kakee,
  (*neuter*) kako
bag tsahnda
baggage aposkevess

bait dholoma
baked pseetoh
baker fournahrees
bakery fournos
balcony balkonee
ball bahla
ballet bahlettoh
ball-point pen steelo
Band-Aid **hahn**saplast
　or lefko**plast**
bank trahpeza
banker trahpezeetees
banknote hartonomeesma
baptism vah**ft**isma
bar bar
bartender barmahn
barbecue **mee**a skara
barber's koureeo
bargain *noun* (good price) efkay**ree**a;
　(agreement) seemfoneea
bargain *verb* napazarepso;
　I don't want to bargain. Dhen **thelo** na pazarepso.
bargaining toh pazah**ree**
barrel varelee
barreled wine **hee**ma krahsee
base vahsee
basement eepoghio
basin neepteera
basket kalathee
basketball **bah**sket
bathe (to) na kahno bahnio
bathroom (with bath) **bahnio** *or* **loutro**;
　(toilet) tooahleta
batik bahteek

battery bahtahreea;
   batteries bahtahree-ess
battle mah-hee
bay kolpos
BC pro Hreestoo (*written as:* π.χ.)
be: to be na eemay; **I will be** tha eemay ;
   I won't be dhen tha eemay.
beach paraleeah;
   nudist beach paraleeah yemniston
beads hahndress;
   worry beads komboloee
beans (dried) fasolia;
   green fasolakia
beard moosee
beautiful (*male*) orayos;
   (*female*) oraya; (*neuter*) orayo
beauty omorfiah *or* orayohtita
beauty parlor komoteerio; komosees
because yatee
become: to become na yeeno
bed krevahtee ;
   single bed mono krevahtee;
   double bed dheeplo krevahtee
      I'm going to bed. Pao ya heepno.
bedbugs koriee
bedroom krevahtokahmera
bee melissa
beef vodheeno
beetroot pantzahree
before preen
begin (to) na arheeso;
   When does it begin? Poteh arheesee?
beginning arhee;
   in the beginning steen arhee

behind (*prep*) pee**so**;
   backside oh peesinohs
believe: I believe (you). (Seh) peestevo.
below kahtoh
bell *church* kampahna;
   door, goat, etc. koodhoonee
belly dance horohs tees keeliahs
belt zonee
beside (*next to*) dheepla
best: the best (*male*) oh pioh kahlos;
   (*female*) ee pioh kahlee; (*neuter*) toh
      pioh kahlo
better kahleetera
better: I feel better. Aysthenomay kahleetera.
Bible, the oh Veevlos
bicycle podheelato
big (*male*) megalos;
   (*female*) megalee; (*neuter*) megalo
bill (check) lohgariasmos
binoculars heeahlia
bird poolee
birth yenisee
birth certificate pistopee-eetiko yeneeseh-ohs
birth control elegos yeneeseh-on
birth control pills ahndisiliptika
birthday: my birthday ta yenethliah mou
biscuit biskotess
bit. a bit ena komatee
 a little bit leegakee
bite (*noun*) **animal** dhagoma; **to eat** boukiah
bite (*verb*) na dhagono
bitter peekro
black mah**v**ro
black market mah**v**ree ahgorah

blanket couverta
bleed (to) na hahno ayma
blind teeflos
block (city) tetragono
blond (*male*) ksanthos;
  (*female*) ksanthee; (*neuter*) ksantho
blood ayma
blood group ohmadha aymatos
blue bleh; galanos
blues ta bloos
board *plank* saneedhee
board (*verb*) epivayno
boat varka; ship pleeo;
  fishing boat kaeekee;
  motor boat venzeenakatos;
  rowboat varka meh koupiah;
  sailboat varka meh panee
body soma
boil (to) na vrazo;
  Should I boil it? Prepee na toh vrazo?
boiled vrasto
bomb bomba
bone kokalo
book vivleeoh
bookshop vivliopoleeo
boot bota
boots botess
border seenoa
bored: I am bored. Variemay.
born: I was born in... Yeneethika stee...
borrow (to) na dhaneesto
boss (*noun*) ahfentiko
both kay ee dheeoh
bottle boukalee; **a bottle of water (wine)**

ena boukalee nehro (krasee)
bottle opener ahneekteeree
box koutee
boy ahgoree
boyfriend feelos *or* ahgahpeemenos
bra soutien
bracelet vra-heeohlee
brake frehno
brandy koniahk
brazier mahngahlee
bread psomee
break down: My car has broken down.
Toh aftokinitoh mou eekheh meea vlavee.
break (*rupture*) **reek**si;
(*pause*) dhee**ah**lima
break (*verb*) na **spah**so
breakfast pro**ee**no
breast stee**th**os
breast feeding veezagma
bride nee**fee**; **bridegroom** gambros
bridge yefira; *card game* breezt
bring (to) na feh**r**ro
Britain Vreetaneea
British (*male*) Vretanos;
(*female*) Ahn**glee**dha; (*neuter*) Vretaniko
brooch karfeetsa
broom skoopa
brother adhelfos
brought effera
brown cafeh
brush voortsa; **paint brush** peenello
bucket kouvas
build (to) na kteezo

building kteerio
bulb *light* lahmpa
bull tahvros
bullet sfayra
bureau grafeeoh;
  Tourist Bureau Grafeeoh Toorismoo
burn (*noun*) engavma; **to burn** na kahpso
  to be burned kayoh
bus leh-oforeeoh
bus station stathmos leh-oforeeon
bus stop stasi leh-oforeeoo
business epiheerisi
businessman epiheerimateeas
busy: The line is busy. Meelaee.
but ahla *or* mah
butane canister feeahlee gahzee
butcher's kreh-ohpoleeoh
butter vooteero
butterfly petaloodha
button koombee
buy (to) na agorahso
Byron Oh Veeron
Byzantine Veezanteeno

C

cabin kahbeena; **single** monokleeno;
  double dheekleeno
cacao kakao
café kahfehneeo
caffeine kahfeh-eenee;

decaffeinated horees kahfeh-eenee
caique ka-eekee
cake kayk
calculator arithmomee-hanee
calendar eemerologhio
call *telephone* teelehfoneema;
  yell (to) fonazo
calm *sea* bonahtsa
camera fotografikee mee-hanee
campsite kataskeenosi
can: I can Boroh;
  I can't Dhen boroh.
can *tin* kootee
can opener ahneekteeree
Canada Kahnadha
Canadian (*male*) Kahnadhos;
  (*female*) Kahnadheh-za
canal kanalee
cancellation ahkeerosi
cancer karkeenos
candle kehree
candy karamelah
canister: butane canister
  feeahlee gahzi
canvas moosama
cap *hat* kahpelo
captain kahpetanios
car ahmaksi
carbonated anthrakiko;
  non-carbonated dhee-hos anthrakiko
card *business* episkepteerio
cards *playing* trapouloharta
card game hartopekseea
carnival karnivahlee;

Carnival Season Ahpokree-**ess**
car park **park**ing
car spare parts ahndalaktika
cargo forteeo
carpenter marangos
carpet halee
carry (to) na seekoso
carton koutee
cashier tahmeeas
casserole yoovetsi
cassette kasetta
castle **kah**stro
cat **ga**ta
catch (to) *fish, etc.* na piahso;
   trains, etc. na prolavo
catholic katholiko;
   Catholic church katholikee ekliseea
caution prosohee
cave speeliah
cd player see-**dee**
cd see-**dee**
cemetery nekrotafeeo
center **ken**tro
century ay-ohnas
ceramics keramika
certain seegoura
certainly vevayos
certificate pistopee-**itikon**
chain ahleeseedha
chair karekla
chamomile hamomeelee
change *coins* pseela
change (to) na ahlahkso
change money na ahlahkso **hree**mata

channel kahnahlee
charter (to) *boat, etc.* na navloso
cheap fteeno
check *bank* tsek
check (to) tsekaro
cheese teeree
chemist's farmakeeo
chess skahkee
chest *body* steethos; *box* keevotio
chewing gum tseekless
chicken kotopoulo
child paydhee
children paydheeah
chips *Britain* patatess teeganitess;
   U.S tseeps
chocolate sokolahta
choose (to) dheealehgo
Christ Oh Hreestos
Christian (*male*) Hreestianos;
   (*female*) Hreestianee
Christianity Hreestianismos
Christmas Hreestooyena
church ekleeseea
cigar pooro
cigarettes tseegara
cigarette papers   hartaki tseegara
cinema seenema
cistern sterna
citizen poleetisi peekoos
city polees
city center kentro
civil war emfeelios polemos
class thesee
classical klasikoh;

Classical Greece arhay-oh Elladha
clean (*adj.*) katharo
clean (to) na kathareeso
cleaners pleenteerio
cleaning, the toh katharisma
cleaning woman kathareestria
climate kleema
clinic kleenikee
clock roloee;
    alarm clock kseepniteeree
close (to) na kleeso
closed kleesto
cloud seenefo
clouds seenefa
cloudy seenefiah
clutch *auto* ambrag-yahz
coast paraleeah
coat *men's* sakahkee;
    woman's zahketta
cockroaches katsareedhess
cocoa kahkao
coffee kafess; **with milk** meh gala;
cognac koniahk
coins nomeesmata *or* kermata
cold (*adj.*) kreeoh
cold (*head*) kreeolohg-yima
color hroma
colleague seenah-dhelfos
college kolleghio
column kolona
columns koloness
comb kteenee
come (to) n'artho
come here! Ella dhoh!

comfortable ahnetoh
Common Market Kinee Ahgorah
Communism komoonismos
Communist komoonistees
companion seendrofos
company *business* etayreea;
  friends pareh-a
complaint parapono
composer seenthetees
computer kompiootehr
concert seenavleea
concussion dheeahseesi
condition katastasi
condom profilaktiko
confectionery store zaharoplasteeo
conference dheeahskepsi
congratulations! sing-hariteeria!
connection seendhesee
constipation dheeskiliothtees
constitution seentagma
consulate prokseneeon
contact lens fakos epafees
continue (to) na seeneheezo
contraceptive andisiliptikoh
contract seemvolayo
convenient: Is it convenient? Volevee?
cook (*noun*) **mahg**-yeeras
cook (to) na magyeerepso
cooker koozeena
cookies beeskota
cool dhrosero
copper halkos
copy (*noun*) ahndeegrafo
copy (to) na ahndeegrapso

cork *bottle* poma *or* fellos
corkscrew teerbooson
corner goneea;
   on the corner stee goneea
cosmetics kaleendika
cost: How much does it cost? Poso kosteezi?
cot kooketta
cotton bambahkee
cough (*noun*) veeha
country *nation* patreedha
countryside eksohee
couple (*noun*) zevgaree
court *law* dheekasteerio
cousin (*male*) ksadhelfos;
   (*female*) ksadhelfee
cove leemnakee
cover (*noun*) couvehrta
cracked (defective) raghismeno
craftsman tehnees
crash *auto* singrousee;
   crash helmet krahnos
crazy (*male*) trehlos;
   (*female*) trehlee
cream krehma
credit card peestotikee karta
crime englima
cross (*noun*) stavros
crossroads stavrodhromee
cruise krou-ahsee-era
cruise ship krou-ahsee-eropleeo
cup fleetzanee
cupboard doolapee
cure (*noun*) therapeea
current revma

customs *border* teloneeoh
customer pelatees
cut (to) na kopso
cut off: The electricity has been cut off.
    Toh **revma eh**-hee kopee.

D

daily (*adverb*) **ka**teh **meh**ra
damaged halasmeno
dance (*noun*) horos
dance (to) na horevo
danger keendinos
dangerous epikeendhino
Danish *(adj.)* Dhanikoh
darling: my darling ahgapee mou
date eemeromineea
daughter koree
dawn (*noun*) avghee
day mehra
  the day after tomorrow methahvrio
  the day before yesterday prokthess
dead (*male*) nekros;
   (*female*) nekree; (*neuter*) nekro
deaf koufos
dear *beloved* (*male*) ahgapitos;
   (*female*) ahgapitee
death thanatos
debt kreh-os
decide (to) na apofaseeso
deep: How deep is it? Poso vathiah?
delay (*noun*) kathistehrisee

democracy dheemokrateea
dentist odhondeeatros
deodorant ahposmeetiko
department store megahlo katasteema
desk grafeeo
dessert epidhorpio
devil oh dheeahvolos
diagnosis dheeagnosi
diamond dheeahmandee
diarrhea dheeahria
dice zahree
dictator dhiktatoras
dictatorship dhiktatoria
dictionary leksiko
die (to) na pethano
diet dhee-eta
difficult dheeskolo
dining room trapezareeah
dinner yevmah
diplomat dheeplomatees
direct kaht'eftheeahn
directions oh-dhigyee-ess
director *business* dhee-eftheentees;
  theater skeenothetees
directory katalogos
dirty vromiko
disaster katastrofee
disco dheesko
disease ahrosteea
distant makreeah
district periohee
dive vootoh
divide horeezo *or* meerazo
divorce dheeazeeghio

dizzy *(male)* zalis**men**os;
(female) zalis**men**ee
do (to) na **kah**no
do not...! mee!
doctor yia**tros**
dog s**kee**los
doll kou**kla**
dollar dho**laree**
dollars dho**laria**
donkey ga**eedhar**os
door **por**ta
doorlock kleedha**riah**
double *twice* **dhee**plo
double bed **dhee**plo kreva**tee**
double room **dhee**klino
down **kah**toh
dowry **pree**ka
drain: The drain is stopped up.
Oh o-hetos eenay kleesmenos.
draw (to) na skedhi**ah**zo
dream *noun* oh**nee**ro;
sweet dreams! oh**nee**ra **glee**ka!
dress *(noun)* fo**re**ma
dressed: to get dressed na dhee**no**may
drink *(noun)* po**toh**
drinking water **po**simo ne**hro**
drive (to) na o**dhee**go
driver o**dhee**gos
driver's license dhee**plo**ma
drugstore farma**kee**o
Dutch *(male)* O**lan**dhos;
(female) Olan**dheh**za
duty: customs duty **for**os

E

e-mail ee-mayl
each katheh
each other kathenas mas
eagle ayetos
ear aftee
early enorees
earrings skoolareekia
earthquake seesmos
earthenware peeleena
east anatolee
eastern anatolikos
Easter Paskha
Easter bread tsoorekee
Easter egg Paskalino avgo
Easter Sunday Kiriakee tou Ahyou Paskha
easy efkolo
eat (to) na fao
economist eekonomolohgos
egg avgo
election eklo-yee
electrical eelektiko
electrical appliances eelektrikess seeskevess
electrical goods store eelektrika eedhee
electric current revma
electrician eelektrologos
electricity eelektrismos
elevator ahsansehr
embarrassed: I am embarrassed.

Vreeskomay seh ahmee-ha**neea.**
embassy presveea
emergency ahnahnghee
empty *(adj.)* **ah**dheeo
end telos
engaged *(to marry)* *(male)* aravonias**men**os;
  (female) aravoniasmenee
engine mee-hanee
England Ahgleea
English *(male)* **Ahn**glos; *(female)* Ahn**gleed**ha
engraving
enough arhetoh
entrance **ee**sodhos
envelope fahkelos
epileptic *(male)* epileeotikos;
  (female) epileeotikee
eraser goma
espadrilles skeenenia papootsia
Euripides Evripeedhess
Europe Evropee
European Evropaeeko
evening vrahdhee
evil: the evil eye toh kako **mah**tee
exactly ahkrivos
examination eksetasi
excavation anaskafee
exchange:foreign exchange seenalagma
excursion ekdhromee
excuse me! seegnomee
exhibition ek**t**hesi
exit eksodhos
expensive ahkrivo
expenses eksodha
export: I export Eksago

express *train* taheea
express *mail* espress
extension (visa, holiday, etc.) paratasee
extension cord epimeeheendiko kalodhio
extra ekstra
eye mahtee
eyeglasses yahliah
eyewash koleerio

F

face prosopo
factory ehrgostasio
faint *(verb)* leepotheemo
   I fainted. Leepotheemisa.
fake pseftiko
fall *autumn* ftheenoporo
family eekooyenia
famous *(male)* feemismenos;
   (female) feemismenee; *(neuter)* feemismeno
fan ahnemisteeras
fan belt looree
far mahkriah;
   How far? Poso mahkriah?
fare, the ta nahvla
farm farma
farmer yeh-orgos
fashion modha
fast greegora ;
   not so fast! O-hee tohso greegora!
fasting: I am fasting. Neestevo.
fat *(adj.)* *(male)* pahees;

(*female*) pahiah; (*neuter*) pahee;
    to get fat paheno
fat (*noun*) leepos
father pahtehras
faucet vreesee
fault: It's my fault. Eenay sfalma mou.
favor, a meea hahree
fax *noun* fahks
feast day yortee
feel (to) na esthanomay;
    How do you feel? Pohs esthaneseh?
ferry fehree boht
fever peeretoh
fiancee (*male*) aravoniastikos;
    (*female*) aravoniastikiah
field horahfee
fight *quarrel* kahvgas
fill: Fill it up. Yemiseh toh.
Film feelm
film-maker kinematografistees
filter (*noun*) feeltro
filtered meh feeltro
filterless horees feeltro
fill (to) na yemeeso
filling in forms seempleerono
find (to) na vroh
finger dhakteelo
finish (to) na teliohso
fire fotiah
first class protee thesee
fish (*noun*) psahree
fish (to) na psahrevo
fisherman psahrahs
fishing psahrevma

fishing boat psahrovarka
fish market psarago**rah**
fish net dheektee
fix (to) na episkevaso
flag seemaya
flashlight fahkos
flea market paliazeedhika
fleas pseelee
flight pteesee
flippers vatrakhopehdhila
floor *of a room* **patoma**
floor *of a building* **o**rofos
florist's anthopoleeo
flour ahlevree
flower louloudhee
flu greepee
flush: It won't flush. Dhen travaee.
Fly (*noun*) **meeg**ha
fly (to) na taksi**dh**epso ah-ehroporikos
folk dance laeekos horos
folk music demotikee moosikee
food fah-ghitoh
foot podhee
football podhosfero
footpath monopahtee
for yiah; **for me** yiah mena;
  for you yiah sena
forbidden ahpagoreveteh
foreign kseno
foreigner (*male*) ksenos;
  (*female*) ksenee; (*neuter*) kseno
forest dahsos
forever yiah **pahn**da
forget (to) na ksekno;

Don't forget! Mee ksekhasees!
fork *for eating* peeroonee
form *official* enteepo
fortress fortessa
forwards embros
foundation eedreema
fountain seendrivahnee
fox ahlepoo
fragile efthrastoh
frame *picture* korneeza
free ellefthero; *gratis* tsamba
freedom elefthereea
freighter fortego
French (*male*) Gahlos;
  (*female*) Gahleedha; (*neuter*) Gahliko
fresh *not stale* fresko;
  fresh today seemerino
fresh water gleeko nehro
fridge pseegheeo
fried teegahnitoh
friend (*male*) feelos; (*female*) feelee
front *adverb* brostah
frontier seenora
frozen kahtapseegmeno
fruit foota
fruit juice heemos footon
fuel kavseema
full yematoh
full moon paselinos
funeral keedheea
funnel honee
funny komiko; *strange* parahkseno
fur goona
furnished epeeplomeno

furniture eepeepla
fuse ahsfahlia;
   The fuse is blown. Kaeekeh ee ahsfahlia.
future, the toh mellon

G

gale thee-ela;
   gale warning anagheleea thee-elees
gallery peenakotheekee
gallon gahlonee
gamble (to) na payzo *or* na pekso
game paykneedhee
garage gahrahz
garden keepos
garlic skordho
gas *cooking* gahz
 for car venzeenee
gas bottle feeahlee gahzee
gas station venzinahdhiko
gate peelee
general *(adj.) yeniko*
general store pandopoleeo
German *(male)* Yehrmanos;
   (female) Yehrmaneedha; *(neuter)* yehrmaniko
Germany Yehrmaneea
get (to) na fehro
get up (to) na seekhonomay
gift dh
girl koreetsee; *young lady* kopella
girlfriend feelee
give (to) na dhoso

give me dhos mou
glass *the substance* yahlee
glass (of water) poteeri (nehro)
glasses *spectacles* yahliah
glue kohla
go (to) na pao; **let's go!** Pahmeh!
goat kahtseekee
God Oh Theh-ohs
goddaughter vaptisteera
godfather nonohs
godmother nonah
godson vaptisimiohs
gold (*noun*) hreesohs
gold leaf feelo hreesou
gold-plated epihreesomeno
good kahlo; **good!** Kahla!
Good Friday Megahlee Paraskevee
good luck! Kahlee tee-hee!
good bye! Ahndeeo *or* Yasoo
 or Sto kahlo
government keevehrneesee
gram gramario
grandchild engonee
grandfather papoos
grandmother ya-ya
grapes stafeelia
grated treemeno
grave *noun* tahfos
greasy *food* leeparo
Greece Elladha
Greek (*male*) **Elleenas**;
 (*female*) Elleeneedha
Greek *language* Elleenika
grill skara; **grilled** tees skaras

grocery store bahkahliko
ground *adj.* treemeno
ground meat keemahs
group group; *of friends* pareh-a
guarantee *(noun)* engyee-eesee
guard *(noun)* feelakas
guest *(noun)* episkeptees
guide *(noun)* odheegos
  tourist guide ksenagos
guidebook odheegos
guitar keethara
gum *chewing* tseekless
gun oplo
gynecologist yeenay-kologos
gypsy *(male)* tseeganos;
    (male) tseegana

H

hair mahliah
hairbrush voortsa mahlion
haircut koorema
hairdresser komotria
hair dryer seswahr *or* peestolahkee
half meeso
ham zambon
hammer sfeeree
hand hehree;
    second-hand metaherismeno
handbag tsahnda
handicrafts heerotek-neea
handkerchief mahndeelee

handsome ohmorfos
hangover *No such concept in Greek!*
happy (*male*) efteekhismenos;
    (*female*) efteekhismenee
harbor leemahnee
harbor master leemenarhees
hard sklero; *difficult* **dheesk**olo
hardware seedherika
harpoon kamakee
hat kahpello
have: I have Eh-ho
he aftohs
head kefahlee
headache ponokefalo
health eegyeea
hear (to) na ahkoso
hearing aid ahkoostika varikoeekas
heart kardhiah
heart attack emfragma
heat (*noun*) ee zestee
heater thehrmastra
heat (to) na zesteno
heaven ooranos
heavy vahree
heel *foot* ftehrna; *shoe* takoonee
helicopter eleekoptero
help *noun* voeethia
hell kolahsee
hello! yasoo!
helmet kranos
herb votano
Hercules Oh Eeraklees
here ehdho
here it is! Nahtoh!

hero eero-ahs
hers dheeko tees
hire (to) na eneekeeahso
his dheeko tou
historian eestorikos
historical eestoriko
history eestoreea
hitch-hike kahno auto stohp
hold (to) na krateeso
hole treepa
holiday eh-ortee
holy (*male*) ahyos;
  (*female*) ah-yeea; (*neuter*) ahyo
home speetee
homemade speeteesio
Homer Oh Ohmeros
homosexual (*male*) omofeelofeelos;
  (*female*) omofeelofeelee
honest (*male*) endimos; (*female*) endimee
honey melee
hope *noun* elpeedha
hospital nosokomeeo
hospitality filokseneea
hostel (youth) ksenonas neh-ohtitos
hot zestoh
hot water zestoh nehro
hotel ksenodho-heeo
hour ora
house speetee
how pohs
how are you? Pohs eesay?
how do you do? Hayreteh.
how far? Poso mahkriah?
how many? Poso?

how much? Poso?
humidity eegraseea
hungry: I am hungry. Peenao.
hurry! Greegora!
hurt: it hurts! Ponaee!
husband ahndhras

I

I ehgo
Icarus Oh Eekaros
ice pahgos
ice-cream pahgo
icon eekona
idea eedheh-a
identity papers taftohteeta
ill (*male*) **ahr**ostos; (*female*) ahrostee
illegal paranomo
imitation ahpomeemisee
important spoudhay-oh
impossible ahdheenato
incense leevahnee
independence ahneksartiseea
indigestion dheespepseea
infection mohleensi
information pleeroforee-ess
ingredients seestaktika
initials monografee
ink melahnee
injury travma
insecticide endomoktohno
instant steegmeeay-oh

institute eedreema
insurance: medical insurance ahsfahlia eegheeahs
insurance policy ahsfalisteerio
insured ahsfalismeno
interest: It interests me. M'endheeahfehree.
Interesting endheeafehron
interior esoteriko
international dhee-ethnees
Internet toh Eenternet
interpreter dhee-ermeeneh-ahs
interval dheeahleema
introduce (to) na seesteeso
introduction seestasees
invite (to) na kahlesso
Ireland Eerlandheea
Irish (*male*) Eerlandhos; (*female*) Eerlandhehza
iron *for clothes* seedhero
iron (to) na seedheroso
is there?/are there? Eeparhee?
Island neesee
Israel Esraeel
Israeli (*male*) Esra-eelinos; (*female*) Esra-eelinee
it aftoh
Italian (*male*) Eetalos; (*female*) Eetaleedha
Italy Eetaleea
itch fagoora
itinerary dhromologhio

J

jack *car* greelos
jacket zahketta
Japan Yahponeea
Japanese (*male*) Yahponehsos;
 (*female*) Yahponehsa
jelly fish tsouktra
Jesus Oh Yeesoos
jetty molos
jewelry kosmeemata
Jewish (*male*) Evray-os;
 (*female*) Evray-a
job dhooliah
joke ahsteeo
journalist dheemosiograhfos
journey tahkseedhee
joy, a meea hara
juice heemos
junta hoonda
justice dheekayoseenee

K

kebab souvlahkia
keep (to) na krateeso
keepsake entheemio
kerosene kahtharo petrelayo
key kleedhee
kilo keelo; **kilos** keela
kilometers heeleeohmetra
kill (to) na skotohso
king vasileh-efs

kiosk pehreeptero
kiss feelee;
    Kiss me! Feeleeseh mou!
kitchen koozeena
knee gonato
knife mahk-heh-ree
knit (to) na pleko
knot kombohs
know(to) na ksehro;
    I don't know. Dhen ksehro

L

labyrinth laveerinthos
lace dentela
ladder skahla
ladies' room toh yeenaykon
lake leemnee
lamb arnee
lamp lahmpa
land *property* kteema
landlady ee speetoh-neekokeera
landlord oh speetoh-neekokeerees
language glossa
lantern fahnaree
laptop computer lahp-top
large mehgahlo
larger peeoo mehgahlo
late argah
later argoteera
laundry pleenteerio
law nomos

law court dheekasteerio
lawyer dheekigoros
leak (*noun*) dheeafeeghee
learn(to) na matheno
lease (*noun*) **mees**thosee
leather *noun* **dherma**
leave (to) na feego
left *adverb* ahreestehra
leg po**dhee**
lend (to) na dhaneeso
lens fahkos
Lent Sarakostee
lesbian lesveea
less leegotero
lesson matheema; **lessons** matheemata
letter grahma
liar pseftees
library veevliotheekee
license *official permit* ahdheea;
   driver's **dhee**ploma
lie *noun* psema
lie down(to) na ksaploso
life zoee
lift *elevator* ahsenserh
lift (to) na seekoso
light *noun* fohs
light (to) na ahnapso
  Do you have a light? Eh-heteeh fotiah?
lighter ahnapteeras
like sahn; **like this** sahn aftoh
like: I like M'ahrehsee
lips heelee
lipstick krahyon
liquid eegro

liter leetro; liters leetra
little meekro; a little leego
live (to) na zoh
live (to) *stay* na meeno
loan (*noun*) dhanio
local topikoh
lock (*noun*) kleedhariah
lock (to) na kleedhoso
look for psahkno
look! Keetah!
lost: I lost. Ekhasa.
lost: I am lost. Eh-ho hathee.
lot, a lot pohlee
loud dheenatoh
love ahgahpee;
   My love! Ahgahpee mou!
love: I love you. S'ahgahpo
love: to make love
   na kahnoomeh ehrota
low hahmeelo
luck teehee:
   Good luck! Kahlee teehee!
luggage ahposkevess
lunch *noun* yevma

M

machine mee-hahnee
magazine periodheekoh
maid eepeeretria
mail ta-heedhromeeo
mailbox gramatokivotio

main square kentrikee plahteea
make (to) na **kah**no
make-up kaleendika
man ahndhras
manager dhee-ef-theen-**dees**
many pohlee; **too many** pahrapolee
map hartees
marble marmaro
market ahgora
marriage gahmos
married (*male*) pahn-dreh-**men**-os;
   (*female*) pahn-dreh-**men**-ee
Mary, Virgin Ee Panag-yeea
matches speerta
material eefasma
matter:It doesn't matter. Dhen peerahzi;
   What's the matter? Tee seemvaynee?
mattress stroma
maybe eesohs
mayor dheemarhos
mean: What does it mean? Tee enoee?
meat kreh-ahs
mechanic meehanikos
medicine farmaka
medieval mess-ay-oniko
medium *sweet, etc.* **meh**trio
meet (to) na seenanteeso
meeting seenahndeesi
menu menoo *or* kahtahlogos
message meenima
meter *taxi* rolo-ee
middle toh **meh**so
midnight meesaneekta
midwife mahmee

milk gahla
mind: I've changed my mind. Ahlaksa gnomee.
mine *adj.* dheeko mou
mineral water metaliko nehro
minister *government* eepourgos
ministry eepouryeeon
Ministry of Agriculture Eeporgheeo Yiorgheeas
Ministry of Defense Eeporgheeo Ahmeenees
Ministry of Education Eeporgheeo Paydheeas
Ministry of Foreign Affairs Eeporgheeo Paydheeas
Ministry of Health Eeporgheeo Eeghees
Ministry of Home Affairs Eeporgheeo Esoterikon
Ministry of Justice Eeporgheeo Dhikayoseenees
Ministry of Transport Eeporgheeo Singinoneea
minute, a ena leptoh
minus pleen
miracle thavma
mirror kathreptees
Miss Dhespeenees
miss: I will miss... Tha mou leepsees....
miss, to *not catch* na hahso
mistake lathos
Mister Keerios
mixed ahnameekta
mobile phone foretoh teelehfono; selular
model *fashion* modelo
modem   modem
modern mohderhno
moment sateegmee
monarchy mohnarheea
monastery mohnasteeree
money hreemata
money order taheedhromikee epitagyee
monk kahloh-yeros

month meena
moon fengahree; **full moon** pahnselinos
more perisotero
morning proee
mosque tzamee
mosquitoes koonoopeea
mother mahna
motorbike motopodheelatoh
motorcycle motoseekleta
mountain voono
mountain climbing orivaseea
mouse pondeekee; **mice** pondeekia
mousetrap fahka
moustache moostahkee
mouth stoma
mouthwash gargara
movie feelm; **movie theater** cinema
Mr. Keerios
Mrs. Keeria
much: too much para pohlee
mud lahspee
mule moolahree
muse moosa;
   The Nine Muses Ta Enneh-a Moosess
museum mooseeo
music moosikee
must prepee
my dheeko mou
myth meethos
mythology meethologheea

N

nails pro**ke**ss; *finger* **nee**heea
nail-clippers neehoko**ptees**
naked *masculine feminine neuter*
name **oh**noma ;
   My name is... Toh onoma mou ee**nay**... ;
   What's your name? Toh onoma sou?
name day yor**tee**
nap ee**nah**kos
napkin pet**se**ta
narrow ste**no**
nation **eth**nos
national ethni**kos**
natural feesi**koh**
navy, the toh nafti**koh**
near kon**da**
necessary ahpa**ray**titoh
neck lay**mos**
necklace koh**lieh**
necktie gra**vah**ta
need: I need hree**ah**zomay
needle ve**lo**na
neighbor yee**to**nas
never po**teh**
New Year kay**noo**rios **hro**nos
New Zealand Neh-a Zeelan**dhee**a
new **neh**-oh
news, the ta **neh**-ah
newspaper efeemeh-**ree**-dha
next eh**po**meno;
   next week teen ah**lee** ev-dho-**ma**-dha
next to **dhee**pla
night **neek**ta; **good night!** kah**lee** **neek**ta;

    tomorrow night ahvrio toh vradhee
nightclub kabareh
nightmare efeealtees
no oh-hee *or* oy-hee
noise thoreevo
non-stop ahnev stathmoo
noon mesimehree
no one kahnenas
normal kahnoneeko
north voriahs
Northern Ireland Voree-eh Eerlan-dheea
not dhen *or* mee oh-hee; **Don't!** Mee!
not enough oh-hee arketoh
notary public seemvolayografos
notebook tetrah-dheeo
nothing teepotah
novel meethistoreema
now torah; **right now** ahmessos
number *street, telephone* arithmohs;
   all others numbers noomero
nun kalogria
nurse nosokomos
nut *food* kahreedha;
   for a bolt pahksimadhee

O

oars koopiah
obligation eepohrehosee
occupation ehpahngyelma
octopus htapodhee
of course vevayos

Odysseus Oh-dhee-seh-efs
Odyssey, the Ee Ohdheesia
Oedipus Oh Eedheepoos
off *turned* kleestoh
office grahfeeo
officer *of the law* ahstinomos
office worker eepahlilo grafeeo
official *government, bank, etc.* eepahlilos
oil lah-dhee
okay endahksi *or* kahla
old (*male*) paliohs;
(*female*) pahliah; (*neuter*) pahlioh;
How old? Pohso hronon?;
I am...years old. Eemay...hronon.
old city pahliah polees
olives eliess
olive oil elayoh-ladoh;
olive tree elayoh-dhentro
Olympic Games, the Ee Oleempiakee Ahgoness
or Ee Oleempia
Olympus Ohleempos
on *(top of)* pahno sto;
switched on ahneektoh;**on time** steen ora tou
once meea fora
one-way street monodhromos
one-way ticket ahplo eeseeteerio
only mono
open ahneektoh
open (to) na ahneekso
opener ahneekteeri
operation egyeerisi
operator teelehfoneetria
opposite (*preposition*) ahpenandeh ahpo
optician optikos

or ee
order sth. (to) na parangheelo
oregano reeganee
oriental ahnatoleetiko
Orpheus Oh Orfeh-efs
Orthodox orthodhokso
Orthodox Church, the
 Ee Orthodhoksos Ekliseea
our; ours dheeko mahs
out; outside ekso
overcoat paltoh
owl kookoovah-ya

P

pack (to) na pahketaro
package dhema
padlock louketoh
pain pohnos
painkiller pafseepono
paint *noun* bohya
painter zograhfos
painting peenakas
pair zevgahree
pants pantalonee
palace pahlatee
paper hartee
paradise pahradheesp
paraffin *kerosene* katharo petrelayo
park *noun* parko
park (to) na parkaro
parliament voolee

parliament building ee voolee
part komahtee
partner seeneeteros
partnership etayreea
party glendee; *political* komma
passenger epivatees
passport dhee-ah-vateerio;
  I lost my passport Ekhasa toh dhee-ah-vateerioh mou;
  My passport has been stolen. Mou klepsaneh toh dhee-ah-vateerio.
passport number ahrithmos dhee-ah-vatireeoo
past, the toh parelthon
patch (*noun*) bahloma
path monopahtee
patience eepomonee
patient (*noun*) ahsthenees
patriarch pahtriarhees
pay (to) na pleeroso
peace eereenee
peanuts feesteekia
pearl margareetaree
peasant (*noun*) horiahtees
pediatrician paydhee-ahtros
pen steelo
pencil moleevee
people kosmos
pepper peepehree
performance parastasees
perfume ahroma
perhaps eesohs
person ahnthropos
personal prosopiko
pet katikeedhio zo-oh

petrol *gasoline* venzeenee
pharmacy farmakeeo
philosopher feelosofos
phone (*noun*) teelehfono
  cellular phone sellular
photocopy (*noun*) fototipeea
photograph (*noun*) fotografeea
photograph (to) na vgahlo fotografeea
photographer fotografos
picture eekona
pie peeta
pier molos
pill hahpee
pillow mahksilaree
pillow case mahksilarotheeki
pilot peelotos
pin karfeetsa
pipe *tube* soleena
pipe *smoking* peep
pistol peestolee
place mehros
plan skehdhio
plate peeahtoh
Plato Oh **Plah**ton
play (*noun*) **ehr**go
play (to) na pekso
playground paydhikee hara
please parakalo
plug *electric* preeza
p.m. meta mesimveeas (M.M. *or* μ.μ.)
pocket zepee
poem peema
poet pee-eetees
poison dheeleeteerio

police ahstinomeeah;
  Tourist Police Tooristikee Ahstinomeeah
police station ahstinomikee tmeema
policeman ahstinomos;
  rural policeman ahgrofeelakos
politician politikos
politics politika
pollution moleensi
pool *swimming* peeseena
poor (*adj.*) (*male*) ftohos;
  (*female*) ftohee; (*neuter*) ftoho
portable foreetoh
portion mereedha
post office ta-hee-dhromeeo
postcard kart postahl
postman ta-hee-dhromos
pottery keramikee
pot *cooking* **heetra;**
  flower pot glahstra
pound *money* **leera;** *weight* **leera**
powder poodhra
power dheenamee
prefer: I prefer Proteemo
pregnant enghios
prepare (to) na eteemaso
prescription seentagyee
president pro-eh-dhros
pressure pee-ehsees;
  high blood pressure eepehrtasi;
  low blood pressure eepotasi
price teemee
pride feelotimo
priest papahs

prime minister protohs eeporgos
prison feelakee
probably pethano
problem prohvleema
profession ehpahng-yelma
professor kathigheetees
promise eepohs-hesees
prophylactic (*noun*) profeelaktiko
prostitute pootahna
publisher ekdhotees
pump (*noun*) ahndleea
puncture (*noun*) treepa
pupil matheetees
purser lohg-eestees
put (to) na **vah**lo

Q

quality peeohteetoh
quarrel *noun* kavgahs
queen vaseelisa
question (*noun*) ehrotima
quickly greegora
quiet eeseeheea

R

rabbit koonellee
rabies leesa
radio rah-dhee-**oh**-fono
railroad see-dheh-**ro**-dromos

railway station stathmos traynou
rain vrohee; **It is raining.** **Vreh**-hee.
rape viasmos
rare spahnio
rat ah-roorayos
rate of exchange teemee seenala**hg**matos
ravine fahrah**ng**hee
raw ohmo
razor kseerahfee
razor blades kseeristi**kess** lepee**d**hess
read (to) na dhee-ah**vah**so
ready (*male*) **eteemos**; (*female*) **eteemee**; (*neuter*) eteemo
receipt ahpodhiksi
reception desk reh-sepsee-**ohn**
recipe seentagyee
recommend: What do you recommend? Tee seeni**stas**?
refill (*noun*) ahdah-laktikoh
refrigerator pseegheeo
registered mail seestimeno grahma
relative singyenees
reliable ahksiohpeestoh
religion threeskevma
remember (to) na theemamay
remind me! **thee**meeseh mou!
rendezvous randehvoo
rent (*noun*) eneekio
rent (to) na eneekeeahso
repair (to) na episkevaso; **Can you repair this?** Boreeteh na toh episkevaseteh aftoh?
replica panomiohpitoh
representative ahdiprosopos

reservation: I have a reservation.
Eh-ho kleesimo.
reserve (to) na kleeso
rest (to) na ksekouras-tho
restaurant estiatoreeo
result (*noun*) ahpotelesma
Resurrection *of Christ* Ee Ahnastasis
return (to) *come back* na yeereeso;
give back na epistrepso
return ticket eesiteerio m'epistrofess
reward ahmivee
rich (*male*) **ploo**sios;
(*female*) **ploo**siah; (*neuter*) **ploo**sio
right ahreestera
right! sostoh!
right-wing dheksiah
ring *finger* dhak-tee-lee-dhee;
engagement, wedding vehra
river potahmee
road dhromos
road map ohdhigos hartees
rob: I was robbed. Meh leepstepsan.
robbery leesteea
robe rohba
rock vrah-hos
Roman roma-ee-koh
roof skepee
room dhomahtio;
double room dheeklino;
single room monoklino
rope skeenee
rose tree-ahn-dafeelo
route dhromologhio*t*
rowboat varka meh kouiah

rug halee
Russia Rooseea

S

sack sakoola
sad (*male*) leepimenos;
  (*female*) leepimenee
safe ahkeendheeno
safety pin paramana
sail (*noun*) pahnee
sailing eestioploeea
sailor naftees
saint (*male*) **ahg**-yos;
  (*female*) **ahg**-yah
salad salata
salt ahlatee
same: the same toh eedheeo
sand ahmos
sandals sahndhalia
sandwich **sahnd**-wits
sanitary ee-yee-ee-**noh**;
  sanitary napkins sehrvee-eh-tess
Santa Claus **Ahg**-yos Vaseelees
sardines sardhel-ess
sausage lookahniko
save (to) na soso
saw *noun* preeohnee
saw, I eedha
say (to) na poh;
  How do you say...? Pohs leneh...?
scarf sarpa

schedule *for the day* programma;
  bus, train, ship dhromologheeo
school skholeeo
scissors psaleedhee
scooter vespa
scorpion skorpiiohs
Scotland Scoteea
Scottish (*male*) Scotehzos;
  (*female*) Scotsehza; (*neuter*) Scotsehziko
scotch tape sellotayp
screw (*noun*) veedha
screwdriver katsaveedhee
scuba diving bohteelyes katadheesios
sculptor gleeptees
sculpture gleeptikee
sea thalassa
seafood thalaseena
seashore paraleea
seasickness nafteea
season epo-hee *or* say-sohn
seat katheesma; **seats** katheesmata
sea urchin ah-heenos
second (*adj.*) dheftero
second *noun* leptoh
second class dhefteree thessee
second-hand meta-heh-rismeno
secret, a ena meestikoh
see (to) na vlepo
sell (to) na pooleeso
send (to) na steelo;
  Can you send it to me? Boreeteh na mou toh steeleteh?
sent: I sent it. Toh ehsteela.
separate (*adj.*) horeesta;
  separate beds (rooms) horeesta dhomatia (krevatia);

separate checks horeestee logariasmee
separated *not divorced* en dhee-ah-**sta**see
serious sovahro
service *table* ee peripee-esee
service *auto* seenteerisees
sew (to) na **rah**pso
sex sehx
sexy **seh**ksee
shade skeeah; **in the shade** stee skiah
shallow *water* reekho
shampoo sampooahn
share (to) na meerastoh;
   We'll share it. Tha toh meerastoomeh.
shark kar-hareeas
sharp koftero
shaving cream krema ksi**rees**matos
she aftee
sheep provatoh
sheepskin proviah
sheets sendohnia;
   clean sheets kathara sendohnia
shellfish thalaseena
shepherd vokos
ship pleeo
ship owner pleeokteetees
shirt pookamiso
shish-kebab souvlaki
shoes papootsia
shop (*noun*) mah**gah**zee *or* katah**stee**ma
shop (to) na psoneeso
shower doos
shutters pahndzooria
sick (*male*) **ah**rostos;
   (*female*) **ah**rostee; (*neuter*) **ah**rosto

siesta mesimvreenohs eepnos *or* repoh
sights: I want to see the sights.
  Thelo na vlepo ta aksiotheh-ata.
sign (*noun*) seema
sign (to) na eepograhpso
silk metahksi
silver ahseemee
sin (*noun*) ahmarteea
sing (to) na tragoodheeso
singer (*male*) tragoodheestees;
  (*female*) tragoodheestria
single *not married* (*male*) ahgamos;
  (*female*) ahgamee
single room monoklino
sink (*noun*) nehroheetees
sink (to) na vooliahkso
Sirens Ee Seereeness
sister ahdhelfee
sit (to) na kahtso
size megathos
ski (to) na kahno skee
skin dherma
skin diving eepovreeheeo koleembee
skirt foosta
sky, the oh ooranos
slacks pantalonia
sleep eepnos; **to sleep** na keemeetho
sleeping bag sleeping bag
sleeping car vahgonlee
sleeping pills eepnotika hahpia
sleepy: I am sleepy. Neestazo.
slice, a meea feta
sling *medical* koonia
slippers papootsia

slowly seega
small meekro
smaller pioo meekro
smell, the ee meeroodhiah
smile (*noun*) hamo-yelo
smoke (*noun*) kahonos
smoke (to) na kahpneeso
smoked *meat, etc.* kahpneestoh
snack elafro fagheetoh
snake feedhee
snake bite dhagoma feedheeoo
snow (*noun*) heeohnee
so much tohso
soap sapoonee
soccer podhosfero
socks kaltsess
socket breeza
Socrates Oh Sokrahtees
soda *bicarbonate* sodha;
  sparkling water sodha
soft malako
soldier strateeohtees
sole *shoe* sola
some merika
someone kahpiohs
something kahtee
sometimes kahpoo- kahpoo
somewhere kahpoo
son yiohs
song tragoodhee
soon takheh-os;
  as soon as possible ohso toh dheenatoh greegorotera
sore (*adj.*) ponomeno

sorry! (*Excuse me*) seegnomee; *sympathy, regrets* Leepamay.
soul, the ee psee-hee
soup soopa
sour peekro
south nohtos
southern nohtios
souvenir entheemio
souvenir shop tooristika ee-dhee
Spain Eespaneea
Spaniard (*male*) Eespanos; (*female*) Eespaneedha
spanner klee-dhee
spare tire rehsehrva
speak (to) na meeleeso;
  Do you speak English? Meelateh Ahnglika?
spear *fishing* kamahkee
specialty, the ee spesialiteh
speed taheetita
spell: How do you spell that?
  Pohs grahfeteh aftoh?
spend (to) na ksodhepso
spider ahrahknee
splint nartheeks
spoiled *food, etc.* halasmeno
sponge sfongahree
sponge diver sfongahras
spoon kootahlee
sports spohr
spot *stain* lekess
spring *season* ahneeksi
square: town square plahteea
squall borah
stadium stadheeo

stage skeenee
stamp *postal* gramatohsimo; *official* hartohsimo
star *sky* ahstehree; *movies* stahr *or* vedetta
start, the ee arhee
start (to) na arheeso; **It doesn't start.** Dhen arheesee.
state *political* krahtos
station stathmos
stationer's, stationery eedhee hartopoleeou
statue ahgalma
stay (to) na meeno
staying: I'm staying at... Meno stee...
steal (to) na klepso
steering wheel teemohnee
steps *dance* veemata
steward, the oh kamarotos
stolen: My wallet (passport) has been stolen. Mou klepsaneh toh portofolee (dhee-ah-vateerio).
stools *feces* kenosees
stomach stomahkee
stomach ache stomakho-ponos
stone pehtra
stop *bus* stahsis
stop! stamahta!; **don't stop!** Mee stamatahs!
store magazee
stove somba
straight eftheea
strange parahkseno
stranger ksenos
street ohdhos
strength dheenamee

stretcher ahsthenoforos
strike *from work* ahpergheea
string spangos
strong (*male*) dheenatos;
  (*female*) dheenatee; (*neuter*) dheenatoh
stuck koleemeno
student (*male*) matheetees;
  (*female*) matheetria
study (to) na spoudhaso
success epiteeheea
sugar zaharee
suggest: I suggest Proteeno;
  What do you suggest? Tee proteenees?
suit kostoomee
suitcase vahleetsa
sum sooma *or* seenolo
summer kalohayree;
  last (next) summer
  toh perasmeno (ahlo) kalokayree
sun, the oh eelios
sunblock cream ahnti-eeliakee krema
sunflower eelios;
  sunflower seeds eeliosporee
sunglasses yaliah eeleeoo
sunstroke eeleeasee
suntan mahvreesma ahpo ton eelio
sunscreen *see* **sunblock**
super market soopehr market
surname ehponimo
surprise ekpleeksi
sweater pullohvehr *or* fahnela
Sweden Sweedheea
Swede (*male*) Sweedhos;
  (*female*) Sweedheza

sweet gleekoh
sweet, a ena gleekoh
swim (to) na koleembeeso
swimming pool peeseena
swimsuit mahyo
Swiss (*male*) Elvetos;
   (*female*) Elveteedha
switch (*noun*) dheeakoptees
sympathy seempatheea;
   My sympathies! Tee seeliptiriah mou!
symphony seemfoneea
synagogue seenagohgyee
system seestima

T

table trapehzee
tablet tahbleta; **tablets** tahbletess
tackle *fishing* eedhee psarikees
take (to) na pahro;
   Can you take me? Borees na meh pahrees?
take off, the ee ahpoyeeosi
talk (to) na meeleeso
tall (*male*) pseelos;
   (*female*) pseelee; (*neuter*) pseelo
tampons tahmpon
tank *water, petrol, etc.* depozitoh
tap *faucet* vreezee
tape *general* tayneea
tape *cassette* kahseta
tape (to) na kahno meea engrahfee
tape-recorder magnetohfono

taste (to) na dhokimahso
tasty nostimo
tavern tahvehrna
tax (*noun*) **foros**
tax stamp hartohsimo
taxi tahksee
taxi driver takseetzees
taxi stand stasee taksee
tea tsaee
teach (to) na dhidhakso
teacher (*male*) **dha**skalos;
(*female*) dhaskala
team omahdha
teaspoon koutalaki
teeth dhondia
telecommunications teeleh-peekeenoneea
telegraph office ohteh
telegram teelehgrafima
telephone (*noun*) teelehfono
  satellite (mobile) phone
telephone (to) na teelehfoneeso
telephone center ohteh
telephone directory katalogos
television teeleeorisi
tell (to) na poh;
  tell him/her/me pehs tou/tees/mou
temperature *weather* thermokraseea;
  I have a temperature. Eh-ho peeretoh.
temple naohs
tent skeenee
terrace tehrahtsa
terrible (*awful*) fovehro
test, a meea eksetahsi
thank (to) na efharisteeso

thank you! efharistoh!;
  You're welcome! Parakalo!
theater theh-atro
theft klepseea
their; theirs dheeko tous
then tohteh
there ehkee
there is/are eeparhee
thermometer thehrmometro
thick *liquid* peektoh;
  wood, etc. hondroh
thief kleftees
thin (*male*) ahdheenatos;
  (*female*) ahdheenatee; (*neuter*) ahdheenato
thing pragma; **my things** ta pragmata mou
think (to) na skeftho; **I think...** Peestevo...;
  What do you think? Tee nomeezees?
thinking: I'm thinking. Skeptomay.
thirsty (I am) Dheepsao.
this aftoh
those aftee
thought, a meea skepsi
thought: I thought Skeftikah.
throat laymos
throw away (to) na petahkso
thumb ahndeeheer
thunder vrondee
tick *insect* tseebooree
ticket eesiteerio;
  return ticket met'epistrofees
ticket office theereedha
tide *sea* pahleeria
tie *necktie* gravata
tie (to) na dhehso

tight sfeektoh
tile *clay* kerameedhia;
 enameled plakakee; *mosaic* mosaeeka
time *clock* ora; *period of* kayros;
 What time is it? Tee ora eenay?
 one time meea fora; **many times** poless foress
timetable dhromologhio
tip *gratuity* poorbooahr
tire (*noun*) lastiko
tired (*male*) koorasmenos;
 (*female*) koorasmenee
tobacco kahpnos
today seemera
together mahsee
toilet paper hartee eegheeas
toilet tooahletta;
 men's ahndhron; **ladies** yeenaykon
tomato tomahto
tomb tahfos
tomorrow ahvrio;
 the day after tomorrow meth'ahvrio
tonight ahpohpseh
too *also* ehpeesees
too little pohlee leego
too much pahra pohlee
too many pahra pohla
took: I took it. Toh peera;
 She/he took it. Toh peereh.
tools ehrgaleea
tooth dohndi
toothache ponodhondhos
toothbrush odhondoh-voortsa
toothpaste odhondoh-pasta
toothpick odhondoh-gleefeedha

tour, a meea periodheea *or* ena toor
tourism toorismos
tourist (*male*) tooreestas;
  (*female*) tooreestria
Tourist Police Tooristikee Astinomeea
tow, a meea reemoulkisee
towel petseta
tower peergos
town pohlees *or* hora
town center, the toh kentro
toy peekneedhee
traffic (*noun*) keekloforeea
traffic light fanaree
traffic police trohaya
tragedy trah-gou-dheea
tragic trah-gheeko
trailer trohospeetoh
train trayno
train station stathmos traynou
tranquilizer katapra-eendhiko
translate (to) na metafrahso
translation metafrahsi
translator metafrahstees
transport metafora
trap *mouse, etc.* fahka
travel (to) na taksidhepso
travel agent prahktor taksidheeon
traveler's check traveler's check
treat: It's my treat. Eenay kehrasma mou.
tree dhentro; **trees** dhentra
trip takseedhee
trousers pantalonee
truth ahleethia
try (to) na prospatho

tuna tonnos
Turk (*male*) **Tour**kos; (*female*) Tourkala
Turkey Tourkeea
turkey gahlopoulo
Turkish tourkiko
Turkish delights loukoumia
turn: turn left streepseh dheksiah;
   turn right streepseh ahreestera
twice dheeo foress
typewriter grahfomee-hanee
typical teepeeko
tyre lahstiko

U

ugly (*male*) **ah**skimos;
   (*female*) **ah**skimee; (*neuter*) **ah**skimo
ulcer elkos
Ulysses Oh Oh-dhee-seh-efs
umbrella ombrella
uncle theeohs
uncomfortable ahvolo
Unction, Extreme efhelayon seh
   etimothanatoh
under kahtoh ahpo
understand:I understand. Katalavayno;
   I don't understand. Dhen katalavayno;
   Do you understand? Katalavaynees?
underwear ehsorooha
unfortunately dheesteehos
unhappy (*male*) dheestee-heesmenos;
   (*female*) dheestee-heesmenee

United Nations, the Ta Eenomena Ethnee
United States, the Ee Eenomeness Politee-ess
university pahnepisteemio
unnecessary peritoh
until mehkree
up ehpahno
upside-down ahno-kahtoh *or* ahnapodha
urinate (to) na ooreeso
us mahs; **for us** yia mahs; **with us** mahzee mahs
U.S.A. Oosa
use (to) na hree-simo-pee-eeso
usually seeneethos

V

vacant ahdheea
vacation dhee-ahkopess
vaccination emvolio
valise valeetsa
valley keeladha
valuable poleetimo
vanilla vaneelia
variety peekileea
vase vahzo
vegetable shop manavees
vegetables lahanika
vegetarian (*noun*) hortofagos
vein fleva
Venetian Enetiko
venereal disease afro-dheesio nosima
very pohlee
veterinarian kteeneeatros

via dheeah
video player veedio kasetoh-fono
video cassette veedio kaseta
view, the ee theh-ah
villa veela
village horeeoh
vineyard ahmbellee
vinegar kseedhee
virus meekrovio
virgin parthehna
Virgin Mary Ee Panagheea
visa ahdhia *or* veeza
  or theh-orisees
visit (to) na episkeftho
visitor episkeptees
vitamins vitameeness
volcano eefestio
vomit (*noun*) emetoh
voyage takseedhee

W

wages merokamata
wait: I'll wait. Tha perimeno;
  Wait! Pehreemeneh!
waiter garsohn
wake (to) na kseepneeso;
  Wake me at... Kseepna meh stees...
wake-up call ahfeepnisi
Wales Oo-ahleea
walk, a meea volta
walk (to) na pehrpateeso

wall teehos
wallet portofolee
want: what do you want? Tee thelees?;
  I want Thelo; **I don't want** Dhen thelo
war pohleemos
warm zestoh
watch (*noun*) roloee
water nehro;
  drinkable water posimo nehro
water-ski (to) na kahno thalasio skee
wave keema; **waves** keemata
way: Which way? Ahpo pioh dhromo?
we emees
weak (*male*) ahdheenatos;
  (*female*) ahdheenatee; (*neuter*) ahdheenatoh
wealthy ploosiohs
wear (to) na foresso;
  What shall I wear? Tee tha foresso?
weather, the oh kayros
weather forecast, the ee provlepsi kayroo
wedding gahmos
week evdhomadha;
  last week teen perasmenee evdhomadha;
  next week teen ahlee evdhomadha;
  this week aftee teen evdhomadha
weekend, the toh savatokeeriako
weight, the toh vahros
welcome (back)! kalosorisess;
  You're welcome! Parakalo!
Welsh (*male*) Oo-ahlos; (*female*) Oo-ahleedha
well (healthy) eeghiees
well (*adverb*) kahla
well *of water* peegadhee
west dheetikoh

wet (*adj.*) vregmeno
what tee
what for? yatee?
wheel rodha
when poteh
where poo
wherever: Wherever you want. Ohpoo theless.
which (*male*) piohs; (*female*) piah; (*neuter*) pioh
who (*male*) piohs; (*female*) piah; (*neuter*) pioh
whole ohloklehro
whore pootahna
why yatee
wick feetellee
wide fardhee
widow heera
widower heeros
wife yeenayka
wild ahgreeo
will *future aux* tha
win, to na kehr-dheeso
wind ahnemos *or* ah-ehras
windmill ahnemomeelos
window paratheero
window pane tzahmee
windshield parbreez
windy feesaee
wine krahsee
winter heemonas
wire seerma
wisdom sofeea
wish (*noun*) efhee
wish:I wish Efhomeh
with meh
without horees

witness marteeras
woman yeenayka
womb meetra
won: I won. Enee-heesa;
  You won. Enee-heesess.
wonderful thavmasio
wood kseelo
wool malee
word leksee
work (noun) dhooliah
work (to) na dhoolepso;
  It doesn't work. Dhen dhoolevee.
worker ehrgatees
world, the oh kosmos
worried (*male*) stenohorimenos;
  (*female*) stenohorimenee
worry: Don't worry! Mee stenohoriessay!
worse heeroteroh
wound (*noun*) pleegyee
worth: How much is it worth?
  Poso ahkseezee?
woven eefantoh
wrap (to) na teeleekso
wrench gahlikoh keedhee
write (to) na grahpso;
  Write me! Grahpseh mou!
writer singrafeh-ahs
wrong: You are wrong. Dhen eh-hees dheekayo; **I was wrong.** Dhen eeh-ha dheekayo.
wrong *incorrect* lathmeno

Y

yacht kotero
yard *of building* ahvlee
year hronos; **last year** pehrisee;
  this year ehfetohs; **next year** toh hronoo
yes nay *or* **mahleesta**
yesterday ekthess;
  the day before yesterday prokthess
yet ahkomee; **not yet** oh-hee ahkomee
YMCA Hahn (**X.A.N.**)
YWCA Hehn (**X.E.N.**)
yogurt yaoortee
Yom Kippur Eemehra Eksilasmoo
you *plural/formal* eh**sees**
you *singular/informal* eh**see**
young (*male*) **neh**-os;
  (*female*) **neh**-ee; (*neuter*) **neh**-oh
your; yours *plural/formal* dheeko sahs
your; yours *singular/informal* dheeko sou
Youth Hostel ksenonas neh-ohteetohs

Z

Zeus Oh Zehfs
zipper fermooahr
zero meedhen
zodiac zodheekos keeklos
zoo zo-olog-yikos keepos

ENGLISH-GREEK

PHRASEBOOK

1. ETIQUETTE

Hello! (*plural/formal*)	**Yasas!**
Hello! (*singular/informal*)	**Yasou**
How are you? (*plural/formal*)	Tee **kanete?**
How are you? (*singular/informal*)	Tee **kanees?**
Fine, thank you.	Kala, efharistoh.
Good morning!	**Kalee mehra!**
Good afternoon!	**Hay**reteh!
Good evening!	**Kalee spehra!**
Good night!	**Kalee neekta!**
See you (*formal/plural*) **tomorrow!**	Tha seh (sahs) **dho ah**vrio!
Goodbye!	An**dee**o!
Bon voyage!	Kalo tak**seed**hee!
Welcome! (*plural/formal*)	Kalosorisess!
Welcome! (*singular/informal*)	Kalosor**ee**seteh!
yes	nay
no	oh-hee
maybe	**ee**sos
thank you	efharisto
good luck!	**kalee teek**hee!
excuse me!	seeg**no**mee!
may I?	boro?
sorry!	seeg**no**mee!

2. QUICK REFERENCE

I	ehgo
you *singular*	ehsee
he/she/it	aftohs/aftee/aftoh
we	ehmees
you *(plural/formal)*	ehsees
they	aftee
this *male/female/neuter*	aftohs/aftee/aftoh
that *male/female/neuter*	ehkeenos/ehkeenee/ehkeeno
these *male/female/neuter*	aftee/aftess/aftah
those *male/female/neuter*	ehkeenee/ehkeeness/ehkeena

here	ehdho
there	ehkee
where?	poo?
who? *(male/female)*	peeohs/peeah?
what?	tee?
when?	poteh?
which? *male/female/neuter*	peeohs/peeah/peeoh?
how?	pohs?
why?	yatee?
how far?	pohso mahkriah?
how much?	pohso?
how many?	pohsa?
what's that?	tee eenay aftoh?
is there?/are there?	eenay?/ eenay?
(does there exist?	eeparkhee?)
how near?	pohso konda?
where is?/are?	poo eenay?/poo eenay?
what must I do?	tee prepee na kahno
what do you want?	Tee theleteh?

(*singular/informal*	Tee **thelees**?)
very	polee
and	kay
or	ee
but	ahla *or* mah
I like/want...	M'ah**ress**ee/**Thel**o...
I don't like/want...	Dhen m'ah**ress**ee/Dhen **thel**o...
I know.	**Kseh**ro.
I don't know.	Dhen **kseh**ro
Do you understand?	Katala**vayn**eteh?
(*singular/informal*	Katala**vayn**ees?)
I understand.	Kata**lav**ayno.
My condolences.	Tees silipitiriah mou.
I am grateful. *male/female*	Eemay ef**hah**ristos/ef**hah**ristee
It's (very) important.	**Ee**nay (polee) spoud**hay**o.
It doesn't matter.	Dhen pee**rah**zee.
No problem!	Dhen **ee**nay **prov**leema!
more or less	**lee**go pohlee
here is/are	**nah**to eenay/**nah**to eenay
Is everything OK?	**Oh**la eenay en**dahk**see?
Danger!	**Keen**dhinos! (ΚΥΝΔΙΝΟΣ)
How do you spell that?	Pohs **graf**eteh af**toh**?
I am....	**Ee**may...
angry *male/female*	thee**omo**menos/thee**omo**menee
happy *male/female*	eftee-hees**men**os/eftee-hees**men**ee
sad *male/female*	leepee**men**os/leepee**men**ee

tired *male/female*	kouras**men**os/kouras**men**ee
well *male/female*	eeghi-**ees**/eeghi-**ees**
cold	Kree**oh**no.*
hot	Zes**tath**ika.
hungry	Pee**nah**oh.
sleep	Nees**tah**zo.
thirsty	Dheep**sah**oh.
worried	Stenohori-**em**ay.

I am right. **Eh**-ho **dhee**kayo.
(Lit. "I have right.")

*In Greek, one often does not use the verb "to be" plus an adjective to describe a state of being. Rather, a verb is employed. Thus, to translate literally from the Greek, "I am cold" becomes "I cold".

3. INTRODUCTIONS

What is your name?		Pohs seh **len**eh?
		(Lit. "How are you said?")
My name is...		Meh **len**eh...
(e.g. My name is Nikos		Meh **len**eh Niko.)
May I introduce you to...		**Bor**oh na seh sees**tee**so
		seh...
This is my...*	*male*	Af**tohs ee**nay oh.....mou.
	female	Af**tee ee**nay ee.....mou.
	neuter	Af**toh ee**nay toh.....mou.
friend	*male*	**fee**los
	female	**fee**lee
colleague	*male*	seenadhel**fos**
	female	seenadhel**fee**
companion	*male*	seendro**fos**
	female	seendro**fos**
relative	*male*	singye**nees**
	female	singye**nees**

*In Greek all pronouns agree with the gender of their noun. Some nouns, however, do not change their endings to express the fact that the person being talked about is male or female. See **Grammar**, pg. .

ABOUT YOURSELF...
NATIONALITY

Where are you from?	Ah**po** poo **ee**seh?
(*plural/formal*	Ah**po** poo **ee**steh?)
I am from...	**Ee**may ah**po**...
(*masculine/feminine/neuter*	ton/teen/toh)
Australia	teen Ahstra**lee**a
Great Britain/England	teen Megah**lee**

	Vretan**eea**/teen Ahng**lee**a
Canada	toh Ka**na**dha
Ireland	teen Eerlan**dhee**a
New Zealand	teen **Neh**-a Zeelan**dhee**a
Northern Ireland	teen Vor**ee**o Eerlan**dhee**a
Wales	teen Oo-ah**lee**a
Scotland	teen Sko**tee**a
the USA	tees Eeno**me**ness Poli**tee**-ess
Europe	teen Ev**ro**pee
India	tees Een**dhee**-ess
Japan	teen Ee-apo**nee**a

I am	**Ee**may...
American *male/female*	Ameri**kah**nos/ Amerika**nee**dha
Australian *male/female*	**Ahf**stralos/**Ahf**straleza
English *male/female*	**Ahn**glos/Ahn**glee**dha
Canadian *male/female*	Kah**nadh**os/ Kah**nadh**eza
Irish *male/female*	Eerlan**dhos**/ Eerlan**dheza**
Welsh *male/female*	Oo-ah**los**/Oo-ah**lee**dha
Scottish *male/female*	Skot**seh**zos/Skot**seh**za

Where we you born? *(plural/formal*	Poo yen**ee**thikess? Poo yenee**thee**keteh?)
I was born in... *(male/female/neuter)*	Yen**ee**thika (ston/steen/sto)...

OCCUPATIONS

What do you do?	Tee dhooleeah **kah**nees?
(plural/formal	Tee dhooleeah **kah**neteh)?
I am (a)*...	Eemay...
academic	akadheema-eekos
accountant	loghistees
actor	eethopiohs
administrator	dhiaheeristees
agronomist	agronomos
archeologist	arhay-ologos
architect	arheetekton
artist	kaliteknees
artist (painter)	zografhos
business person	emborikos
carpenter	marangos
consultant	embeerognomon
dentist	odhondheeatros
diplomat	dheeplomahtees
director	dhee-eftheentees
(stage, film	skeenothetees)
doctor	yiatros
economist	eekonomologos
engineer	mee-hanikos
farmer	yee-orgos
film-maker	kineematografhistees
guide	oh-dheegos
(tourist guide	ksenagos)
journalist	dheemosiografhfos
lawyer	dheekeegoros
manual worker	ergahtees
mechanic	mee-hanikos
negotiator	dhee-a-pragmatevtees
nurse *male/female*	nosokomos/nosokoma

office worker	gramate**fs**
photographer	foto**grah**fos
professor *male/female*	kathig-ee**tees**/ kathi**gee**tria
pilot	pee**lo**tos
scientist	he**ti**kos epis**tee**mon
secretary	gramate**fs**
(**private** *male*	eedhee-**ay**teros
female	eedhee-ay-**teh**-ra)
student *male*	spou-dhas**tees**
female	spou-**dhas**-treea
surgeon	hee-roor-**gohs**
teacher *male/female*	**dha**skalos/**dha**skala
tourist*male/female*	too**rees**tas/too**rees**tria
writer	singra**fefs**

*The indefinite article is never used when speaking of one's profession, e.g. "I am pilot" = **Eemay peelotos**. Also, the form often remains the same regardless of the sex of the person being spoken about.

AGE

How old are you?	**Po**son hro**non ee**say?
(*plural/formal*	**Po**son hro**non ee**steh?)
I am...years old.	**Ee**may...hro**non**.

FAMILY

Are you married? *male/female*	**Ee**say pahn-dreh-**me**nos/ pahn-dreh-**me**nee?
I am single. *male/female*	**Ee**may **ah**gamos/**ah**gamee.
I am married. *male/female*	**Ee**may pahn-dreh-**me**nos/ pahn-dreh-**me**nee.

I am divorced. *male/female*	Eemay horismenos/horismenee.
I am widowed.	Heerevo.
Do you have a boyfriend?	Eh-hees feelos (agapeemennos)?*
Do you have a girlfriend?	Eh-hees feelee (agapeemennee)?*

*Inasmuch as "feelos" and "feelee" can also mean simply "friend," if you wish to be quite specific, you should use the terms "agapeemenos" and "agapeemenee" (lit. "loved one"), although these, in turn, are, to Greek ears, rather personal. Other terms are "gomenos" for "boy friend" and "feeleenah-dha" for "girl friend," but these have their origin in gutter slang and can be thought very coarse.

What is his/her name?	Pohs ton/teen leneh?
How many children do you have?	Posa paydhiah eh-heteh?
I don't have any children.	Dhen eh-ho paydhiah.
I have a daughter.	Eh-ho meea koree.
I have a son.	Eh-ho enas yohs.
How many sisters do you have?	Pohsess ah-dhelfess eh-heteh?
How many brothers do you have?	Pohsa ah-dhelfia eh-heteh?

father	patehras
mother	meetehra
grandfather	papoos
grandmother	ya-yah
brother	ah-dhelfos
sister	ah-dhelfee

godfather	nonohs
godmother	nonah
aunt	theeah
uncle	theeos
children	pay-dheeah
daughter	koree

son	yohs
twins	**dhee**-dheema
husband	**ahn**-dhras
wife	yee**nay**ka
spouse	**see**zigos
family	eekouyenia
man	**ahn**-dhras
woman	yee**nay**ka
boy	ahgoree
girl	kor**tee**si
young lady	ko**pel**la
person	**ahn**thropos
people	**ahn**thropee

RELIGION

Since the final schism in 1054 between the Roman and Eastern churches over papal authority, Greece has been fiercely and proudly Orthodox, with the church playing a leading role in many of the most significant political events in Greek history, particularly the revolution against the Ottoman empire. It is the official state religion, and one professed by nearly an absolute majority of Greeks. While there are small pockets of Catholics, Jews and Muslims (most of the latter left over from the 1922 population exchange with Turkey), they cannot be said to be welcomed with open arms.

What is your religion?	Tee **ee**nay ee three**see**a sahs?
I am (a) ...	**Ee**may...
Muslim	Moosel**mah**nee
Orthodox	Or**tho**doksos
Christian	Hree-sti**a**nos
Jewish	Evray-os
Islam	Ees**lam**
Christianity	Hreestiah-nees**mos**
Judaism	Ee-oo-dha-ees**mos**
I am not religious.	Dhen **ee**may **threes**kos.

4. LANGUAGE

Since the acceptance of Greece in the EC in 1981, the study of English as a second language has become increasingly common so that now most Greeks in the thirties and younger speak at least a smattering of the language. Interestingly, the names of most automobile parts are derived from the French, the first car in Greece having been a Renault. Some German is also spoken because a large number of Greeks go and did go to the country as workers. In addition, since the collapse of the Communist empire, there has been a large influx of Russian and Eastern European speaking Greeks who have only a rudimentary knowledge of Greek.

Do you (*plural/formal*) **speak...**
   English?
   French?
   German?
   Russian?

Meelahs (Meelateh)...
   Ahglika?
   Gahlika?
   Yermanika?
   Roosika?

Does anyone speak **English?**
I speak a little...
I don't speak...
I understand.
I don't understand.

Kanenas meelaee Anglika?
Meelao leega...
Dhen meelao...
Katalavayno.
Dhen katalavayno.

Please point to the word in the book.

Parakalo, **dheekseteh** teen **leksee** sto vivleeo.

Please wait while I look up the word.

Parakalo, perimeneteh na **psakn**o na vro teen leksee.

Could you speak more slowly, please?

Tha bor**eeteh** na meelateh peeoo seegah, parakalo?

Could you repeat that?	Tha boreeteh na toh ehpanalaveteh?
How do you say... in Greek?	Pohs to lehneh... stah Ellenika?
What does...mean?	Tee seemaynee....?
How do you pronounce this word?	Pohs teen proferees aftee tee leksee?
I speak...	Meelao...
Danish	Dhanika
Dutch	Olandika
English	Ahglika
French	Galika
German	Yermanika
Italian	Eetalika
Japanese	Yaponesika
Norwegian	Norvighika
Russian	Rosika
Swedish	Soo-ee-dhika
Turkish	Tourkika

5. BUREAUCRACY

Most tourist-oriented forms are written in Greek and English and/or French and can be filled in in those languages. Business forms, etc. are usually only in Greek. Thus the details below are purely for reference purposes.

FILLING IN FORMS

surname	επώνυμο (**eponimo**)
given name	όνομα (**ohnoma**)
full name	ονοματεπώνυμο (onomate**ponimo**)
father's name	πατρώνομα (pat**ronoma**)
address	διεύθυνση (dhee-**ef**-theensee)
address abroad	διεύθυνση στο εξωτερικό (dhee-**ef**-theensee sto eksote**ri**ko)
address in Greece	διεύθυνση στην Ελλάδα (dhee-**ef**-theensee steen El**la**dha)
date of birth	έτος γεννής (**etos** yen**nees**)
place of birth	τόπος γεννίσεος (**topos** yen**nee**seh-os)
nationality	υπηκοότητα (eepeeko-**oh**tita
age	ηλικία (eeli**kee**a)
sex: male	φύλο (**feelo**) : άρρεν (**ahren**)
female	θήλυ (**theelee**)
religion	θρησκεία (threes**kee**a) *

*Never asked about on any official form.

reason for travel	σκοπός του ταξειδίου (sko**pos** tou taksi**dee**ou)
business	επιξειρήσεις (epihee**ree**sees)
tourism	τουρισμός (touris**mos**)
work	δουλειά (dhoo**liah**)
personal	προσωπικό (proso**piko**)
profession	επάγγελμα (e**pahn**gyelma)
marital status	συζυγική κατάσταση

(sizigyi**kee** kata**stasi**)

single m.	ανύπαντρος (ahnee**pandros**)
f.	ανύπαντρη (ah**nee**pandree)
married m.	παντρεμένος (pandreh**menos**)
f.	παντρεμένη (pandreh**menee**)
divorced m	διεζευγμένος (dhee-ehzevg**menos**)
f.	διεζευγμένη (dhee-ehzevg**menee**)
date	ημερομηνία (eemeromi**neea**)
date of arrival	ημερομηνία αφίξεως (eeromi**neea** ah**feek**se-ohs)
date of departure	ημερομηνία αναχώρησης (eeromi**neea** anaho**ri**sees)
passport	διαβατήριον (dhiava**tee**rion)
passport number	αριθμός διαβατηρίου (arith**mos** dhiavati**ree**ou)
visa	βίζα (**vee**za) *or* θεώρηση (theh-**o**risi)
residence permit	άδεια παραμονής (**ah**deea paramo**nees**)*
currency	νόμισμα (**no**misma)
foreign	συνάλλαγμα (see**na**lagma)

*This is what the Greeks call what we usually refer to as a "visa". Its initial length varies according to the particular agreement made between Greece and other countries. After that, extensions - usually easy to get - have to be applied for.

MINISTRIES

Ministry of Defense	Υπορyείο Αμύνης (Eepor**ghee**o Ah**mee**nees)
Ministry of Agriculture	Υπορyείο Γεωργίας (Eepor**ghee**o Yior**ghee**as)
Ministry of Home Affairs	Υπορyείο Εσοτερικών

	(Eeporgheeo Esoterikon)
Ministry of Foreign Affairs	Υπορχείο Εξοτερικών
	(Eeporgheeo Exoterikon)
Ministry of Transport	Υπορχείο Συγκοινωνία
	(Eeporgheeo Singinoneea)
Ministry of Health	Υπορχείο Υγείας
	(Eeporgheeo Eeghees)
Ministry of Education	Υπορχείο Παιδείας
	(Eeporgheeo Paydheeas)
Ministry of Justice	Υπορχείο Δικαιοσύνης
	(Eeporgheeo Dhikayoseenees)
Ministry of Public Order	Υπορχείο Δημοσίας Τάξης
	(Eeporgheeo Dheemoseeas Tahksees)
Ministry of Shipping	Υπορχείο Ναυτιλίας
	(Eeporgheeo Naftileeas)
Ministry of Commerce	Υπορχείο Εμπορίου
	(Eeporgheeo Emboreeou)
Ministry of Tourism	Υπορχείο Τουρισμού
	(Eeporgheeo Toorismou)
Greek National Tourist Organization	Ελληικός Οργανισμός Τουρισμού
	(Ellinikos Organismos Tourismou)*
Tourist Police	Τουριστική Αστυνομία
	(Tooristikee Astinomeea)

*But always referred to by its acronym, E.O.T (pronounced "Eh-**oht**")

USEFUL PHRASES

Is this the correct form?	Aftoh eenay toh sostoh endipo?
What does this mean?	Tee seemaynee toh aftoh?

Where is the office of...	Poo **eenay** toh gra**fee**eo tou...?
Which floor is it on?	Seh **pee**on **o**rofos **ee**nay?
Does the lift work?	Dhoo**le**vee toh ahsan**sehr**?
Is Mr./Mrs/Miss....in?	O **Kee**rios/Ee Kee**ree**a/ Ee Despi**nees**...**ee**nay **meh**sa?
Please tell him/her that I am here.	Paraka**lo**, pess tou/tees poo **ee**may e-**dho**.
I can't wait. I have an appointment.	Den bo**roh** na peri**me**no. **Eh**-ho rendeh**vou**.
Tell him/her that I was here.	Pes tou/teen poo **ee**mouna eh-**dho**.

6. TRAVEL

Public transport - Greece has an excellent bus system both within and between cities and towns. Trains are generally slow, expensive and subject to inscrutable delays. All forms of transportation are horribly crowded during peak summmer months, particularly ships, so tickets should be purchased as far in advance as possible. With ships, delays and cancellations because of the weather, especially in winter, are to be expected. Motorbikes can be rented almost everywhere.

ENQUIRIES

What time does (the)...leave/arrive?	Tee **ora fevghee/fthanee** (toh)....?
the airplane	toh ah-ero**plah**no
the boat	toh **plee**o
the bus	toh leh-oh-fo**ree**o
the train	toh **tray**no
the trolleybus	toh **troh**lee
It is delayed.	**Eh**-hee kathiste**hri**see.
It is cancelled.	Ahkee**ro**thi.
How long will it be delayed?	Yia **poh**so kay**ro** tha **eh**-hee kathiste**hri**see?
There is a delay of …..hours.	**Eh**-hee … **or**ess kathiste**hri**si.
Excuse me, where is the ticket office/ travel agency?	Seeg**no**meen, poo **ee**nay tee thi**ree**dha/toh prakto**ree**o taksi**dhee**eon?
Where can I buy a ticket?	Poo bo**roh** na ago**ra**zo eesee**tee**rio?
I want to go to...	**The**lo na **pa**o stee...*
I want a ticket to...	**The**lo eesee**tee**rio yia tee..
I would like...	Tha **ee**thela...
a one-way ticket	ah**plo** eesee**tee**rio

a return ticket	met'epeestro**feess**
first class	pro**tee thess**ee
second class	**dhef**teree **thess**ee
third class	tree**tee thess**ee
business class	emborikee **thess**ee
tourist class	touristikee **thess**ee
deck class	kata**stroma**
a single cabin	monoklino**
a double cabin	**dhee**kino**

Can I reserve a place?	**Bor**oh na **klee**so **thess**ee?
How long does the trip take?	**Poh**see **ora eenay** toh tah**ksee**dhee?
Is it a direct route?	**Pa**ee kat'ef**thee**ahn?

How do I get to...	Pohs **pao**...
the airport?	sto ah-e**rodh**romio?
the harbor?	sto lee**ma**ni?
the station?	ston stath**mo?**
Do you want...	**The**leteh...
an I.D.?	taf**toh**tita?
my passport?	toh dhee-ah-va**tee**rio mou?

*Since the greater majority of place names are feminine, the use of the feminine form of the preposition "to" ("stee") is always a safe bet. The masculine preposition is "ston" and the neuter "sto".

**These terms also apply to railway sleeping cars and hotel rooms.

AIR

In Greece, all flights are non-smoking. There is an extensive network via Olympic Airways to almost all parts of the country including the larger islands, with various types and sizes of planes. Most flights go through Athens or Thessaloniki, Greece's northern capital and second largest city.

Is there a flight to...?	Eeparkhee pteesee yia tee...?
When is the next flight to...?	Poteh eenay ee epomenee pteesee stee...?
How long is the flight?	Posee ora eenay tee pteesees?
What is the flight number?	Tee eenay oh arithmos tees pteesees?
You must check in at...	Prepee na ftahneteh sto...
Is the flight delayed?	Ee pteesee eh-hee kathisterisi?
How long is the flight delayed?	Yia posee ora ee pteesee tha eh-hee kathisterisi?
Is this the flight for...?	Aftee eenay ee pteesee yia tee...?
Is that the flight from...?	Aftee eenay ee pteesee ahpo tee...?
When is the Athens flight arriving?	Poteh tha fthasee ee pteesee ahpo teen Atheena?
Is it on time?	Eenay steen ora tees?
Is it late?	Eh-hee kathisterisi?
Do I have to change planes?	Prepee na ahlakso ah-eroplahno?
Has the plane left for Athens yet?	Efeegeh to ah-eroplahno ahkoma yia teen Atheena?
What time does the plane take off?	Tee ora anahoree toh ah-eroplahno?
What time do we arrive in Athens?	Tee ora tha fthasoomeh steen Atheena?

airline	ah-eroporikee gramee
airport	ah-ehrodromio
excess baggage	ehpeepleh-on ahposkevess
international flight	dhee-efnee pteesee
internal flight	esoterikee pteesee

BUS

Virtually all municipal buses have ticket machines requiring exact change. The ticket which is then dispensed should be kept ready to show the occassional conductors who board the buses and spot check tickets. Intercity buses leave from terminals situated in that part of the city nearest the exit road for their destination. These terminals are called "praktoreea" ("agencies") in Greek and are often just a table in a cafe or restaurant. Tickets can and should be bought in advance. As noted above, buses are the most dependable form of transportation in Greece and are virtually the only thing in the country that is almost always on time.

bus stop	stasee (ΣΤΑΣΙΣ)
Where is the bus stop/station/agency for...?	Poo eenay ee stasee leh-oforeeou/oh stathmos leh-oforeeon/toh praktoreeo yia tee...?
Take me to the bus station.	Na meh pahteh sto stathmo leh-oforeeou.
Which bus goes to...?	Peeoh leh-oforeeo paee stee...?
Does this bus go to...?	Aftoh toh leh-oforeeo paee stee...?
How often do buses pass by?	Katheh poso perasee leh-oforeea?
What time is the...bus?	Tee ora eenay toh... leh-oforeeon?
next	epomeno
first	proto
last	teleftayo
Will you let me know when we get to...?	Boreeteh na mou peeteh opoteh fthasoomeh stee...?
Stop, I want to get off!	Stamata, thelo na katevo!
Where can I get a bus to...?	Poo boroh na pahro leh-oforeeo yia tee...
When is the first bus to...?	Poteh eenay toh proto

	leh-ofo**ree**o yia tee...
When is the last bus to...?	**Pot**eh **ee**nay toh tele**ftay**o leh-ofo**ree**o yia tee...
When is the next bus to...?	**Pot**eh **ee**nay toh e**pom**eno leh-ofo**ree**o yia tee...
Do I have to change buses?	**Prep**ee na ah**lahk**so leh-of**orree**ah?
I want to get off at...	**Thel**o na ka**tev**o stee...
Please let me off at the next stop.	Paraka**lo** na meh ah**fee**seteh n'**ahv**go steen e**pom**enee **stah**see.
Please let me off here.	Paraka**lo** ah**fee**semeh eh-**dho**.
How long is the journey?	**Poh**see **or**a **ee**nay toh tak**seed**hee?
What is the fare?	**Poh**so kos**tee**zi?
I need my luggage, please.	**Prep**ee na **ekh**o ee ahpo-s**kevess** mou.
That's my bag.	Af**tee ee**nay ee **tsahn**da mou.

SHIP

In Greece, there is nothing less certain than ship departures. Therefore, it is imperative that you check with the port authority and/or your ticket agency several times before giving up your hotel room and trekking down to the port. Delays and cancellations are the rule, particularly during bad winter weather, but also during the summer when the prevailing north wind, the "meltemi" is in full force. Tickets should be bought well in advance, especially during summer when the crush of tourists waiting to travel makes the evacuation of the Titanic look like a family outing. Tickets can be bought at agencies near the port; on some islands these are located in shops and groceries with signs outside advertising which line they are representing. Most ships take cars, but reservations for these should be made as far in advance as possible.

a (the) ship	**en**a (toh) ka**rav**ee *or* **plee**oh
a (the) ferry (for cars)	**en**a (toh) **feh**ree boht

Is there a ship for...?	Eh-hee karaveee yia tee...?
Does it take cars?	Pernee ahmaksi?
I would also like a ticket for my car.	Tha **ee**thela eepee**sees** eesi**tee**rio yia toh ah**mak**si mou.
When does it arrive/leave?	Poteh th'arthee/tha feeghee?
Will it be delayed?	Tha kathisteree**si**?
How many hours/days?	Posess oress/mehress?
Are you sure?	Eesteh seegoros?
From which pier?	Ahpo peeah apovathra?
Where is it?	Poo eenay?
Where is the harbor?	Poo eenay toh leemanee?

TRAIN

Trains are the worst possible choice to make for traveling anywhere in Greece. They are invariably crowded, noisy, hot, and late. Unless, of course, you take first class, particularly on the Athens-Thessaloniki run, where recently-acquired express trains can make the journey short and pleasant. There are two railroad stations in Athens: the "Stahmos Larissa" for Northern Greece, the former Yugoslavia, and Turkey; and the "Stahmos Peloponisou" for the Peloponnese. Both are located on the opposite side of the same tracks near Omonia Square. Tickets can be bought from numerous travel agencies throughout Athens and Piraeus, or at the station, or on the train.

I want to go...	**The**lo na **pa**o...
to Thessaloniki.	stee Thessalo**nee**kee.
the railroad station.	sto stath**mo** tray**nou**
Take me to the railway station.	**Pah**re meh sto stath**mo** tray**nou**.
Where can I buy tickets?	Poo bo**roh** na ago**ra**zo eesi**tee**ria?
I want a sleeping car.	**The**lo vagon-**lee**.

a single	**mono**klino
a double	**dhee**klino
I want the express train.	**Thelo** toh ta**hee**a.
Passengers must...	Ee epivati **prepee**...
change trains.	na ahlak**soon tray**na.
change platforms.	na ahlak**soon** apo**vath**res
Is this the right platform for...?	**Ee**nay af**tee** ee so**stee** apo**vath**ra yia tee...
The train leaves from platform...	Toh **tray**no **fev**ghi ahpo teen apo**vath**ra...
Is there a timetable?	Er**park**hee dhromo**logh**io?
Which platform should I go to?	Stee **pee**ah apo**vath**ra **prepee** na **pao**?
platform one/two	apo**vath**ra **mee**a/**dhee**o
You must change trains at...	**Prepee** na ahlak**seteh tray**na stee...
Will the train leave on time?	Ta **tray**na tha **fee**goun steen **ora** tou?
There will be a delay of ...minutes.	Tha **ekhee**...**lepta** kathiste**hri**si.
There will be a delay of ...hours.	Tha **ekhee** ...**oress** kathiste**hri**si.

TAXI

There are taxis everywhere in Greece, even on the smallest islands. Their color can be different from city to city. Always make sure the meter is turned on when you begin the journey; if there is no meter, negotiate a price in advance; in cities, various prices are often posted in the taxis. There is usually a surcharge to airports, etc. and prices often double late at night. With the exception of Athens, taxis can be stopped and shared with other passengers; this does not, however, mean a reduction in prices, so if the meter is already running, check what it says when you get in: but remember that the final calculation will also involve the base fare. Tips are not expected.

Taxi!	Tah**ksee!**
Where can I get a taxi?	Poo borroh na vro tah**ksee?**
Please could you get me a taxi?	Parakalo, boreeteh na meh pareteh ena tah**ksee?**
Can you take me to...?	Boreeteh na meh **pah**reteh stee...?
Please take me to...	Parakalo, **pah**reh meh stee...
How much will it cost?	**Poh**so tha kos**tee**zee?
To this address, please.	Steen aftee teen dhieftheensi
Please turn on the meter.	Parakalo, ar**khee**steh toh roloee.
Turn left.	Streep**se**teh ah**ree**ste**rah**.
Turn right.	Streep**se**teh dheksi**ah**.
Go straight ahead.	**Pah**teh ef**theea**.
Stop!	Sta**ma**ta!
Don't stop!	Mee stama**tahs**!
I'm in a hurry.	Viah**so**may.
Please drive more slowly!	Parakalo, odhi**ghee**teh pee**oo ar**gah**!
Here is fine, thank you.	Eh-**dho** eenay kala, efharistoh.
The next corner, please.	Teen **ah**lee go**nee**ah, parakalo.
The next street to the left.	Ton **ah**los **dh**romos ah**ree**ste**rah**.
The next street to the right.	Ton **ah**los **dh**romos dheksi**ah**.
Stop here.	Sta**ma**ta eh-**doh**.
Stop the car, I want to get out.	Stama**tee**seteh toh ah**mah**ksi, thelo na katevo.
Please wait here.	Parakalo, peri**me**neteh eh-**dho**.

Take me to the airport.	Pahreh meh sto ah-erodhromio.

GENERAL PHRASES

I want to get off at...	Thelo na katevo stee...
Excuse me!	Seegnomeen!
Excuse me, may I get by?	Seegnomeen, boroh na perahso?
These are my bags.	Aftess eenoon ee dheekess mou valeetsess.
Please put them there.	Parakalo, na tees valeteh ehkee.
Is this seat free?	Aftoh toh katheesma eenay elef-thero?
I think that's my seat.	Peestevo aftoh to katheesma eenay dheeko mou.

EXTRA WORDS

airport	ah-ehro-dhromio
airport tax	foros ah-ehrodhromio
ambulance	ahs-thenoforo
arrivals	ahfeeksees: ΑΦΙΞΕΙΣ
bicycle	podheelato
boarding pass	dhelteeo epivivaseh-ohs
boat	varka
passenger ship	pleeoh *or* karavee
bus stop	stahsee leh-ofoeeou: ΣΤΑΣΙΣ
cancellation	ahkeerosis
car	ahmaksi *or* aftokeenito
4-wheel drive	four-wheel
check-in counter	katagrahfee ahposkevon
check-in	toh check-in
closed	kleesto: ΚΛΕΙΣΤΟΝ
customs	teloneeo: ΤΕΛΩΝΕΙΟ

delay	kathisterisee
departures	anahorisi: ΑΝΑΧΩΡΗΣΕΙΣ
dining car	vagonee estiatoreeoo
emergency exit	eksodhos kindheenoo: ΕΞΟΔΟΣ ΚΙΝΔΥΝΟΥ
entrance	eesodhos: ΕΙΣΟΔΟΣ
exit	eksodhos: ΕΞΟΔΟΣ
express train	ta-heea
ferry	fehree boht
harbor	leemani
helicopter	eleekoptero
information	pleeroforee-ess: ΠΛΗΡΟΦΟΡΙΕΣ
ladies room	toh yeenaykon: ΓΨΝΑΙΚΩΝ
gents	toh ahndrohn: ΑΝΔΡΩΝ
local (for trains)	topikoh
motorbike	motopodheelato
motorcycle	motosikleta
motorscooter	scootehr *or* vespa
no entry	ahpahgorevetay ee eesodhos: ΑΠΑΓΟΡΕΨΕΤΑΙ Η ΕΙΣΟΔΟΣ
no smoking	ahpahgorevetay toh kapneesma ΑΠΑΓΟΡΕΨΕΤΑΙ ΤΟ ΚΑΠΝΗΣΜΑ
open	aneektoh: ΑΝΟΙΚΤΟΝ
path	monopahtee
pier	apovathra
platform number	arithmos ahpovathra
railway	see-dher-rodhromos
reserved	kleesmeno: ΚΛΕΙΣΜΕΝΟ
road	dhromos

seat *or* place	**thess**ee
sign	**see**ma
sleeping car	vahgon-**lee**
station	**stath**mos
telephone	te**leh**fono
ticket office	thi**ree**-dha
timetable	dhromo**lo**ghio
toilets	too-ah-**let**tess
town center	**ken**dro
train station	**stath**mos **tray**nou

7. ACCOMODATION

All hotels except those in the luxury class are price-controlled according to their assigned category. These prices are required to be posted inside the door of the room. If you are one person and find yourself given a double room, ask if you are paying for the entire room or just the bed; certain hotels in the cheaper categories tend to rent beds, not rooms, and you could wake up in the middle of the night to find yourself sharing your precious privacy with a complete stranger.

Greek hotels no longer pay any attention to whether foreign couples are married or not, but they will want to keep one or both of your passports. This is to register you, as required by law, with the local police; it is also to ensure that you do not skip out without paying the bill. In hotels with the bath down the hall, hot showers often cost extra, and one must arrange with the manager beforehand to have the water heater turned on. If you have any problems, go to the local tourist police and let them handle it.

I am looking for a...	Psahkno ena...
guesthouse	pahnsion (*or* rent room)
hotel	kseno-dho-**hee**o
hostel (youth)	ksenonas neh-**oh**titos
I want a room for the night.	**Thel**o dhomatio ya toh **vra**-dhee.
We wants rooms for the night.	**Thel**oomeh dhomatia ya toh **vra**-dhee.
Where is...	Poo **ee**nay...
a cheap hotel	ena ftheeno kseno-dho-**hee**o
a good hotel	ena kalo kseno-dho-**hee**o
a nearby hotel	ena kseno-dho-**hee**o eh-**dho** konda
a clean hotel	ena katharo kseno-dho-**hee**o
What is the address?	Tee **ee**nay ee dhee-**ef**theensi?
Could you write the address, please?	Bor**ees** na teen **grahp**sees, parakalo?

AT THE HOTEL

Do you have any rooms free?	Eh-hee ellefthera dhomatia?
I have a reservation.	Eh-ho kleesimo.
My name is...	Toh onoma mou eenay...
May I speak to the manager, please?	Boroh na meeleeso meh ton dheeeftheedees, parakalo?
I would like...	Tha eethela...
a single room	ena mohnokleeno
a double room	ena dheekleeno
We'd like a room.	Tha eetheloumeh ena dhomatio.
We'd like two rooms.	Tha eetheloumeh dheeo dhomatia.
I want a room with ...	Thelo ena dhomatio meh...
a single bed	ena mohno krevahtee
a double bed	ena dheeplo krevahtee
a bath	bahnio
a shower	doos
hot water	zestoh nehro
breakfast	proeenoh
a television	teeleeorasi
a window	paratheero
a balcony	balkonee
quiet (without noise)	eeseeha (horees thoreevo)
for one night (week)	ya ena vra-dhee (evdhomadha)
for two or three nights	ya dheeo ee treeah vra-dhia
I don't know yet how long.	Dhen ksehro ahkoma ya poso kayro.
Am I paying for the bed room?	Pleerono ya toh krevahtee ee toh dhomahtio?;
I want the entire room only for myself.	Thelo ohlo toh dhomahtio mohno ya mena.
I only want to pay for the bed.	Thelo na pleeroso mohno ya toh krevahtee.

How much is it per night/per person!	Poso kahnee ya **ena** vra-dhee/ya **katheh** ahtomo?
How much is it per week?	Poso kahnee ya teen evdhomadha?
Can I see it?	Boroh na toh dhoh?
Are there any others?	Eeparhee ahla?
Is there...?	Eh-hee...
air conditioning	kleematismo
laundry service	pleenteeria
room service	sehrvees dhomateeoo
a telephone	teelehfono
hot water	zestoh nehro
No, I don't like it.	Oh-hee, dhen m'ahreesi.
It's too ...	Eenay pohlee...
hot	zestee
cold	kreeoh
big	magalo
dark	skotino
small	meekro
noisy	thoreevodhees
dirty	vromiko
It's fine, I'll take it.	Kahlo eenay, toh thelo.
Where is the toilet/bathroom?	Poo eenay ee tooahleta/toh bahnio?
Is there hot water all day?	Eh-hee zestoh nehro ohlee teen eemehra?
Do you have a safe!	Eh-hee kreematokeevotio?
Can I use the telephone!	Boroh na hreesimopee-eeso toh telehfono?

NEEDS

I need...	Hreeahzomay...

candles	kehriah
toilet paper	hartee eegheeahs
soap	sapoonee
clean sheets	kathara sendohnia
an extra blanket	ahkoma meea kooverhta
drinking water	posimo nehro
a light bulb	meea lahmpa

Please wake me up at... (o'clock).	Parakalo, kseepnameh stees... (ee ora).
a wake-up call	afeepnisi
Please change the sheets.	Parakalo, ahlakseh ta sendohnia.
I can't open/close the window.	Dhen boroh na ahneekso/kleeso toh paratheero.
I have lost my key.	Eh-ho hasee toh kleedhee mou.
Can I have the key to my room?	Boroh na eh-ho toh kleedhee ya toh dhomatioh mou?

The water has been cut off.	Ehkopseh toh nehro.
The electricity has been cut off.	Ehkopseh toh revma.
The heating has been cut off.	Ehkopseh tee thehrmansi.
There's no hot water.	Dhen eh-hee zestoh nehro.
The heater doesn't work.	Ee thehrmastra dhen dhoolevee.
The air conditioning doesn't work.	Oh kleematismos dhen dhoolevee.
The phone doesn't work.	Toh teelehfono dhen dhoolevee.
I can't turn off the faucet.	Dhen boroh na kleeso tee vreesee.
The toilet won't flush.	Dhen travaee toh kazanakee.
The toilet is blocked.	Toh kazanakee eh-hee voolosi.
I am leaving now.	Fevgo torah.
We are leaving now.	Fevgomeh torah.

GREEK DICTIONARY AND PHRASEBOOK

I would like to pay the bill.	Tha **ee**thela na plee**ro**so toh lohgarias**mo**.

EXTRA WORDS

bathroom	**loo**troh *or* **bah**nio
bed	re**vah**tee
bill	lohgarias**mo**
blanket	koo**ver**hta
candle	keh**ree**
chair	ka**rek**la
clean	katha**ro**
cold water	kree**oh** ne**ro**
cupboard	doo**lah**pee
dark	sko**ti**no
dirty	vro**mi**ko
doorlock	kleedha**ree**ah
double bed	dhee**plo** krevahtee
electricity	**rev**ma
fridge	psee**ghee**o
hot/cold	zes**toh** / kree**oh**
hot water	zes**toh** ne**ro**
key	klee**dhee**
laundry	**rou**ha ya plee**si**mo
mattress	**stro**ma
meals	yev**ma**ta
mirror	kathrep**tees**
name	**oh**noma
noisy	thorivo**dhees**
padlock	louke**toh**
pillow	mahksi**lah**ree
plug (elec.)	**pree**za
quiet	eeseehee**ah**
room	dho**ma**tio
room number	arith**mos** dhoma**tee**ou

179

shampoo	sampoo**ahn**
sheet	sen**do**nee
shower	doos
suitcase	va**lee**tsa
surname	eh**po**nimo
table	trah**peh**zee
towel	pet**se**tta
water	**ne**hro
window	para**thee**ro

Electric current - Greece has 220-volt electric current, most of it AC, although there may be some DC on parts of the remoter islands. However, the alternating current alternates considerably, varying in strength and subject to sudden and often unexplained blackouts. Flashlights, candles, and lanterns are always good to have around as are good batteries in your laptop and radio.

8. FOOD AND DRINK

The partaking of food and drink, preferably in a large group of friends, is a time-honored ritual in Greece that certainly goes much further back in history than what is probably the world's most famous gathering of this sort, Plato's *Symposium*, when Socrates and friends got together for an evening of drink and talk. One of the delicacies of that period, tiny meatballs called *keftedes*, are still a staple of modern Greek food. Many of the tastiest and most exotic items on the Greek menu, however, were developed during the 400-year rule of the Ottoman Empire and have Turkish names like *moussaka* and *baklava*. It is a matter of hot dispute whether they were originally Greek dishes given Turkish names by their Greek cooks to make the Turks happy or were actually Turkish dishes since taken into the province of Greek cuisine. Whatever, eating and drinking with the Greeks, whether at restaurants and tavernas or their numerous feast and name days is a glorious experience and without a doubt the best way to get to know the country. So dig in – not only to dish your but everybody else's. It's the way it's done!

Some advice: once you've secured your table and gotten the attention of a waiter (often about as difficult as swimming the Hellespont), go with him to the back of the establishment and look at the dishes available. Often there are glass-fronted food warmers and refrigerators sitting there just for this purpose; or, if not, go into the kitchen and peek in the pots. Don't worry – you will be welcome! It is much easier to order this way. You can not only see what it looks like but all you have to do is point. Besides, menus are often highly unreliable indicators of what's really available on that particular day.

MEALS

breakfast	pro-ee**no**
lunch	**yev**ma
snack	ela**fro** fagee**toh**
dinner, supper	**yev**ma
dessert	epi-**dhor**-pio
I'm hungry.	Pee**nao**.
I'm thirsty.	**Dheep**sao.
Lent	Sarakos**tee.**
I am fasting.	Nee**stev**o.

EATING OUT

Do you know a good restaurant?	Ksehreteh ena kalo estiatorio?
I would like a table for ... please.	Tha eethela ena trah-**peh**-zee ya...., sahs parakalo.

Waiter!	Garsohn!
The menu please!	Toh menoo, sahs parakalo.
I've haven't decided.	Dhen **eh**-ho ahpofa**seeseh**.
I would like to order now.	Tha eethela na parangheelo torah.
What's this?	Tee eenay aftoh?
What do you recommend?	Tee seenistahsetay?

Does it have meat in it?	**Eh**-hee kreh-ahs mehsa?
Does it have alcohol in it?	**Eh**-heh eenopnevma mehsa?
Do you have ...?	**Eh**-heteh...?
Can I order some more...?	Boroh na parangheelo ahlo...?
That's enough, thank you.	Ahfta fthanee, efharistoh.
I haven't finished yet.	Dhen **eh**-ho teliohsee ahkoma.

I have finished eating.	**Eh**-ho teliohsi na fao.
I am full up!	Eemay fool!
Where are the toilets?	Poo eenay ee tooahlettess?

I am a vegetarian.	Eemay hortofagohs.
I don't eat meat.	Dhen trogo kreh-ahs.
I don't eat pork.	Dhen trogo heereeno.
I don't eat chicken or fish.	Dhen trogo ooteh kotopoulo ee psahree.

I don't drink alcohol.	Dhen peeno enopnevma.
I don't smoke.	Dhen kapneezo.

I would like...	Tha eethela...

an ashtray	ena tahsahkee
the bill	toh loh-gah-ree-ahs-**mo.**
a glass of water	ena poteeree neh**ro.**
another chair	ahlee meea karekla.
another plate	ahlo ena peeahtoh.
another glass	ahlo ena poteeree.
another cup	ahlo ena fleetzahnee.

Note: The bread, knives, forks, spoons, and sometimes napkins are usually brought to the table by the waiter in a basket. The ensemble is called "the service" -- toh seh**rvee**tsio.

EXTRA WORDS

another	ahkoma
ashtray	tasahkee
bill, the	ton loh-gah-ree-ahs-**mo**
bottle-opener	ahneek**tee**ree
bread	psomee
chair	kahrekla
a corkscrew	ena teer-boo**sohn**
a cup	ena fleetzahnee
dessert	epi-**dhor**-pio
food	fah-ghee-**toh**
fork	pee**roo**nee
glass	poteeree
knife	mak-**hay**ree
lemon	lemonee
mustard	moos**tar**-dha
napkins	petsettess
oil	**lah**-dhee
pepper	peepehree
plate	peeahtoh
portion of, a	mia meh**ree**-dha
salt	ah-**lah**tee

slice of, a	meea feta
table, a	ena trah**pehz**ee
spoon	koo**tah**lee
(for soup)	(tees **soup**ahs)
straw, a	ena kala**mah**kee
sugar	**za**haree
table	tra**pehz**ee
teaspoon	kouta**lak**ee
toilet, the	ee too-ah**let**ta
toothpicks	oh-dhon-doh-gli**fee**-dhess
vinegar	k**see**-dhee
water	**neh**ro
(mineral)	(metaliko nehro)
wine	krah**see**
fresh	**fres**ko
spicy	pee**kahn**-diko
stale	bahg-**ya**tiko
sour	k**see**no
sweet	g**lee**ko
hot	**zes**toh
cold	**kree**oh
salty	al**mee**ro
tasteless	ho**rees yev**see
tasty	**nos**timo
too much	para polee
too little	polee leego
not enough	oh-hee arhetoh

FOOD

APPETIZERS*	OREKTIKA
aubergine dip	melitzanosalata
cheese	tee**ree**

cheese, fried	saga**nah**kee
fish-roe puree	taramosalata
meatballs	kefte-**dhah**-kia
octopus	htapo-**dhee**
olives	eli**ess**
shrimp	ga**ree**dhess
smelts	maree-**dhess**
vine leaves, stuffed	dhol**ma**-dhess
yogurt-garlic dip	zah**tzee**kee

*More commonly called "mehzeh" or "mezedhahkia.

egg, an	ena avgo
fried eggs	avga **mah**tia
omelet	ome**le**ta
bean soup	fasolia **soup**a
egg-lemon-rice soup	avgo-**lem**ono
fish soup	psarosoupa
vegetable soup	hortohsoupa

rice, cooked	peela**fee**
spaghetti	mahka**ro**nia
macaroni pie	pah**steet**sio

beef	vo-dhee**no**
meatballs	kef**teh**-dhess
in tomato sauce	soutzou**ka**kia
in egg-lemon sauce	youvar**la**kia
and-pasta casserole	you**vet**see
chicken	ko**toh**poulo
goat	kat**see**kee
lamb	ar**nee**
pork	heeri**no**
veal	mos**kha**ree

schnitzel	sneetzel
boiled	vrasto
chops	breezoless
grilled	tees **skah**ras
roasted	psee**toh**
spit-roasted	stee **souv**la
shish kebab	souvlakee
stewed	yiak**nee**
fish, a	ena psahree
baked	psahree pseetoh *or* psahree plahkee
fresh	**fres**ko
fried	teegahnitoh
frozen	kahtepsig**meno**
grilled	tees **skah**ras

sauces:
butter-lemon	vootiro**lem**ono **salt**sa
garlic puree	skor-dhal-**ya**
oil-lemon	la-dho-**lem**ono **salt**sa

lobster	ahsta**kos**
mullet (grey)	**kef**alos
(red)	bar**boo**nia
octopus	htapo-**dhee**
shrimp	gah**ree**-dhess
shark	gah**lay**os
smelts	mah**ree**-dhess
squid	kala**ma**ree
swordfish	ksi**fee**ahs
beans (dried)	fasolia ksira

(fresh)	fasolia **freska**
cabbage	**lahk**hano
chick peas	re**vee**thia
eggplant	melit**sah**na
greens	**horta**
okra	**bahm**-yes
peppers	peeperie**ss**
stuffed	yemis**tess**
potatoes	pah**tah**tess
fried	teegahnee**tess**
tomatoes	ta**mah**tess
stuffed	yemls**tess**
vine leaves (stuffed)	dolma-**dhess**
zucchini	koloko**kee**thia
a salad	**mee**a salata
Greek	hori**ah**tikee salata
mixed	ahnah**mik**tee salata
with (without)	meh (ho**rees**)
oil	**lah**-dhee
vinegar	k**see**-dhee
onions	kre**mee**-dhia
oregano	ree**gah**nee
cabbage	**lahk**hano
cucumbers	ahn**goo**ree
lettuce	mah**roo**lee
peppers	peeperie**ss**
tomatoes	to**mah**tess
fruit	**froo**ta
grapes	sta**fee**lia
lemon	le**mo**nee
melon	pe**po**nee
peaches	ro-**dhah**kino

ENGLISH - GREEK PHRASEBOOK

watermelon	karpoozee
dessert	epi-**dhorpia**
yogurt with honey	yaoortee meh **melee**

With the exception of yogurt, desserts (and coffee) are normally not served in any Greek restaurants aside from those in the luxury, international category. One must go instead to a combination confectionary store-and-cafe called a "zakharoplasteeoh".

cake	**keh**-ik
custard	**krema**
chocolate	**krema** sokola**hta**
crême caramel	**krema** karame**leh**
rice pudding	reezogallo
halva	hal**vahs**
ice cream	pago**toh**.
pastries	pah**stess** *or* gleeka tahpsioo

Tipping: For **restaurant waiters** the tip is usually included in the bill. This is indicated on the menu by a double list of prices, the one on the right being the cost of the food plus the tip. However, if the service has been courteous and prompt, it is customary to leave a little something extra. Give this to the waiter by hand, since any money left on the table is considered to be the property of the busboy who sets and clears the tables. For **taverna waiters**, the tip is usually not included in the bill unless the taverna is a luxury one. Therefore, leave about 10-20%, again giving it directly to him. For the **busboy**, leave a small tip on the table, preferably under a plate.

DRINK

beer	**beer**a
brandy	kon**yak**

coffee	kafess
Greek:	Eleeniko:
black, a	ena **skeh**toh kafeh
medium-sweet	ena mehtrio
sweet	ena glike**ev**rasto
iced	Nes**ca**feh fra**peh**
instant	**Nes**cafeh
with milk	meh **gah**la
with sugar	meh **zak**haree
cognac	kon**yak**
juice	hee**mos**
apricot	ve**ree**koko
orange	portoka**lah-**dha
peach	ro-**dhah-**kinou
pineapple	ah**nana**
tomato	tomah**toh**zoumo
lemonade	lemo**nah-**dha
milk	**gah**la
orangeade	portoka**lah-**dha
ouzo	**oo**zo
soda water	so-dha
soft drink	anapsikti**koh**
tea	tsah-ee
chamomile	hamo**mee**lee
tonic water	**toh**neek.
water	**neh**ro
mineral water	meta**liko neh**ro
wine	**krah**see
red	**mah**vro *or* **ko**kino
retsina	ret**see**na
rose	**ro**zeh
white	**ah**spro
dry	**broos**ko
sweet	**glee**koh

barreled heema krahsee

NOTE: Barreled wine is sold by the kilo (or half- or quarter-kilo), a kilo being approximately 1 quart.

Toasts:
Birthday, Name Day	**Hro**nia pola! ("Many years!")
Bottoms up!	**Ah**spro **pah**toh!
Cheers!	**Vee**va! *or* Ehveeva!
To us!	**Ya**mas!
To your health!	Eesi**ghee**a!

9. DIRECTIONS

Where is...?	Poo eenay...?
the academy	ee ahka**deme**ea
airport	ah-e**rodhro**mio
the art gallery	ee pinoko**thee**kee
a bank	ee **trahpe**za
the church	ee ek**lisee**a
the city center	toh **kent**ro
the consulate	toh prok**senee**on
the... embassy	ee....prez**vee**a
my hotel	toh ksena-dho**hee**eo mou
an information office	grah**fee**eo pleerofo**rion**
main square	kentri**kee** plat**ee**a
the market	ee ago**rah**
the Ministry of...	toh eepour**ghee**eo
the mosque	toh **tzah**mi
the museum	toh moo**see**eo
parliament	ee voo**lee**
the police station	toh astino**mi**ko **tmee**ma
the post office	toh ta-hee-dhro**mee**eo
station	stath**mos**
the telephone center	toh teeleh**foni**ko **kent**ro
a toilet	**mee**a too-ah**letta**
university	panepis**tee**mio

What ... is this?	Tee....**ee**nay?
bridge	ye**fee**ra
building	k**tee**rio
district	peri**ohee**
river	po**tah**mee
road	**dhro**mos
street	**dhro**mos *or* **odhos**

suburb	proastio
town	polees
village	horeeoh

What is this building?	Tee eenay aftoh toh kteerio?
What is that building?	Tee eenay ehkeeno toh kteerio?
What time does it open?	Tee ora ahneeghee?
What time does it close?	Tee ora kleenee?

Can I park here?	Boroh na parkaro ehdhoh?
Are we on the right road?	Pahmeh kala?
How many kilometers is it to...?	Posa heeliohmetra eenay stee...?
How far is the next village?	Poso makriah eenay sto epomeno horioh?
Where can I find this address?	Poo boroh na vro aftee teen dhee-efthinsi?
Can you show me (on the map)?	Boreeteh na mou dheekseteh (stoh hartee)?

How do I get to...?	Pohs pao stee....?
I want to go to ...	Thelo na pao stee...
Can I walk there?	Boroh na pao meh ta podhia?

Is it far?	Eenay makriah?
Is it near?	Eenay konda?
Is it far from/near here?	Eenay makriah ahpo/ kondah edhoh?

It is not far.	Dhen eenay mahkriah.
Straight ahead.	Eftheeah.
It's two blocks down.	Eenay dheeo dhromee peeoo katoh.

Turn left.	**Streeps**eteh dheksiah.
Turn right.	**Streeps**eteh ahreesterah.
at the next corner	steen epomenee goneea
at the traffic lights	sta fanariah
behind	**pee**so
far	mahkri**ah**
in front of	brosta ahpo
left	dheksiah.
right	ahreesterah
near	konda
opposite	ahpenandee
straight on	kaht'eftheeah
bridge	yefeera
corner	goneea
crossroads	stavrodhromee
one-way street	monodhromos
south	notiahs
east	ahnatoliko
west	dheetiko
north	vori**ahs**

10. SHOPPING

Dealing with the opening and closing hours of stores is perhaps the most frustrating exoeience you will encounter during your stay in Greece. This is because Greek stores always seem to be closed when you particularly need them open. The reason is rooted in the time-honored, virtually sacred Mediterraneam tradition of the 3-4 hour afternoon siesta, which most Greeks ferociously cling to even in the face of a sagging economy and four horrible rush hours a day. Since Greece's inclusion on the EC, legislation has attempted to create an straightforward 9-5 day, but only Athens has really made an effort to apply it. Thus, anywhere else in the country you will find an incredibly-complicated, staggered system of opening and closing hours.

The only rule of thumb about shopping that can be applied with any certainty is that all stores are usually open in the mornings from about 8-to-1, Monday through Saturday. Figuring out the evening hours is mind-boggling. Whether or not certain stores are open on a particular evening depends both upon the type of store and on the day of the week. It also depends on which city, town or village you are in, since opening and closing hours are regùlated by local governments and traditions, not by any national or even regional scheme.

Fortunately, when in Athens, one can consult the city's excellent English-language magazine, The Athenian, for a table of opening and closing hours for all shops. In other areas, try to do your shopping in the mornings.

If the shops are closed and you desparately need something, there is always a strong possibility you can find it at a kiosk (peh**reep**tero). These seem to have stuffed into them, in a space as confined as the first astronaut's capsule, just about everything one could imagine -and then some: cigarettes, lighters, fluids, gases, flints, sweets, magazines, newspapers, books, shaving creams, brushes, razors and razor blade, combs, detergents, hand soaps, colognes, postage stamps, envelopes, writing paper, postcards, sun glasses,: trãnsistor radios, batteries, pens, pencils, incense, kleenex, deodorants,suntan lotions, bobby pins, bottle openers, prophylactics, and God and its owner know what else. In addition, the majority of them have telephones from which one can make local calls or, if a special meter has been installed, long distance or international calls on the automatic dialing system. They are open seven days a week throughoutthe morning, afternoon and evening. However, most (but not all) of them close around midnight, so be sure to stock up on cigarettes (or whatever else you may need for the wee hours) before then.

shop, a　　　　　　　　　　　　　ena magazee *or* ena katastima

I am going shopping.	Psoneezo.
the shopping	ta psonia.
When are the shops open?	Poteh eenay ahneekta ta magaziah?
Where can I find a...?	Poo boroh na vroh...?
Where can I buy...?	Poo boroh na agoraso...?
Where's the market?	Poo eenay ee agora?
Where's the nearest....?	Poo eenay toh peeo konda...?
Can you help me?	Boreeteh na meh voeetheeseteh?
Can I help you?	Boroh na seh voeetheeso?
I'm just looking.	Keetahzo mono.
I'd like to buy ...	Tha eethela na agoraso...
Could you show me some...?	Boreeteh na mou dheekseteh merika...
Can I look at it?	Boroh na toh dhoh?
Do you have any...?	Eh-heteh...?
This.	Aftoh.
That.	Ehkeeno.
I don't like it.	Dhen m'ahrehsi.
I like it.	M'ahrehsi.
Do you have anything cheaper?	Eh-heteh kati peeoo ftheeno?
cheaper/better	peeoo ftheeno/kaleetero
larger/smaller	peeoo megalo/meekrotero.
Do you have anything else	Eeparhee kati ahlo?
Do you have any others?	Eg-heteh ahlee?
Sorry, this is the only one.	Leepahmay, aftoh eenay toh mohno.
I'll take it.	Tha toh pahro.
How much/many do you want?	Poso theleth?
How much is it?	Poso kahnee?

Can you write down the price?	Boreeteh na **grahp**seteh tee **tee**mee?
Could you lower the price?	Boreeteh na hameeloseteh tee **tee**mee?
I don't have much money.	Dhen **eh**-ho pola **hree**mata?
Do you take credit cards?	**Pehr**neteh peestoti**kess kar**tess?
Would you like it wrapped?	Tha toh dheeleekso?
Will that be all?	Tha eenay **oh**la?
Thankyou, goodbye.	Efharis**toh**, ahn**dee**o.
I want to return this.	**The**lo na toh epis**tre**pso af**toh**?
auto spares store	ahndalaktika
baker's	toh **for**no
bank	**tra**peza
barber's	kou**ree**o
I want a haircut please.	**The**lo ena koo**re**ma parakalo.
bookshop	veevleeopo**lee**o
butcher's	hasa**pees**
pharmacy	farma**kee**o
clothes store	**ee**-dhee ematis**mou**
dentist	odhond**hee**atros
department store	me**ga**lo katas**tee**ma
dressmaker	mod**hee**stra
electrical goods store	ee**lek**trika **ee**dhee
flea market	pali**azee**-dhika *or* yousa**room**
florist	anthopo**lee**o
greengrocer	mana**vees**
hairdresser	komo**tria**
hardware store	maga**zee** poo **poo**laee seed**her**ika
hospital	nosoko**mee**o

kiosk*	peh**ree**ptero
laundry	pleen**tee**rio
market	ago**rah**
newsstand	maga**zee** poo poo**laee** efeemeh**ree**dhess
shoeshop	epodhesmatopo**lee**o
shop	maga**zee** *or* kata**stee**ma
souvenir shop	tooristi**ka** ee**dhee**
stationer's	hartopo**lee**o
supermarket	**soo**pehr **mar**ket
travel agent	**prak**tor taksi**dhee**on
vegetable shop	mana**vees**
watchmaker	rolo**gahs**

GIFTS

Arts & crafts – Greece's arts and crafts are a reflection of its history, many being as old and celebrated as the country itself. The area around the Acropolis was famous for its ceramics even before the Classical era and the luminous art of the Neolithic Cycladic period was a clear forerunner of the unique craftsmanship to be found on sale in the shops of Mykonos and other islands of the area today. Meanwhile both the ubiquitious copies of icons as well as the superb original jewelery available in tourist shops and expensive boutiques are direct descendents of the high art of the Byzantine period. In recent years there has been an explosion of creativity in all areas of the arts and there is consequently a treasure trove of original works waiting in galleries all over the country for the discerning eye and not necessarily very deep pocketbook.

Note: Greek law defines antiquities as anything dating from before 1821. It does not forbid their being purchased by foreigners but it does prohibit taking them out of the country without a required permit, something which could involve years of paperwork and never be resolved. If you have any doubt about the age of something you have puchased, it would be wise not to try to take it out of the country without first checking with the customs authorities. Otherwise, if discovered with a real antiquity, you could end up spending time in an extremely unpleasant jail.

alabaster	ahlavastros
box	koutee
bracelet	vra-hee-ohlee
brooch	porpee
candlestick	kahn-deeleh-ree
carpet	ha-lee
ceramics	keramika
chain	ahliseedha
clock	orologhio
copper	halkos
crystal	kreestalo
earrings	skoolareekia
enamel	smalto
folk (*adjective*)	la-eeko
gold	hreesos
handicrafts	heerotehneea
icon	eekona
iron	seedhero
jade	nefreetees
jewelry	kosmeemata
leather	dhehrma
metal	mehtalo
modern	mohdherno
necklace	kolieh
painting	peenakas
pottery	keramikee
ring	dhak-tileedhee
(engagement, wedding)	vehra
silver	ahseemee
stone	pehtra
tile (enameled)	plakakee
(clay)	kerameedhee
(mosaic)	mosa-eeka
turquoise	tourkooahz

traditional	para-dho-siako
vase	**vah**zo
watch	roloee
wood	kseelo
wooden	kseelino
worry beads	kombolo-ee

CLOTHES   ROUHA

Traditional Greek clothing, which is to say clothing worn mainly by peasants and soldiers at the time of the 19th century uprisings against the Ottoman Empire, varies from area to area. It is still worn today on various national and local feast days and holidays, when communities make it a matter of pride to bring out the clothes of their forebearers who crried the flag of revoltuion against the Turk, and perform dances of the period. Some of these clothes can be bought in antique stores while dolls attired in the costumes are availbale at most tourist shops.

bag	**tsahn**da
bathing suit	mah-**yo**
belt	loo**ree**
boots	**boh**tess
cotton (*adjective*)	bamba**ke**ro
dress	fo**re**ma
gloves	**gahn**dess
handbag	**tsahn**da
hat	kah**pel**lo
jacket	zah**ket**ta *or* saka**kee**
jeans	**tzeen**s
leather	**dhehr**ma
overcoat	pal**toh**
pocket	ze**pee**
scarf	**sar**pa *or* kah**skol**
shirt	poo**ka**miso
shoes	pa**poot**sia
slacks	pahn-ta**lo**nia

socks	**kalt**sess
suit	ko**stoo**mee
sweater	poo**loh**vehr *or* fa**nel**la
T-shirt	fa**nel**la
trousers	pahn-ta**lo**nee
umbrella	om**brel**la
underwear	eh**so**-rooha
wool	mah**lee**

TOILETRIES, ETC.

aspirin	ahspir**ee**nee
bandaid	**han**saplast *or* **lef**koplast
comb	kte**nee**
condom	pro-filak-**ti**ko
cotton	bamba**kee**
deodorant	ahposmeeti**koh**
hairbrush	**voor**tsa
lipstick	kra**hyon**
mascara	mah**ska**ra
mouthwash	gar**gah**ra
nail clippers	neekoko**ptees**
painkillers	ahnalg-**yee**tika
perfume	**ah**roma
powder	**poo**dra
razor	ksee**rah**fee
razorblades	kseeresti**kess** le**pee**dhess
safety pin	para**ma**na
shampoo	sam**poo**ahn
shavingcream	**kre**ma kseer**ees**matos
sleeping pills	eep**no**tika **hah**pia
soap	sah**poo**nee
sponge	sfoon**gah**ree
sunscreen	ahndee-**ee**lia**kee kre**ma
tampons	tahm**pon**

thermometer	thehrmometro
tissues	hartomahn-deela
toilet paper	hartee eegyeeas
toothbrush	odhondoh-vortsa
toothpaste	odhondoh-pasta

STATIONERY — EEDHEE HARTOPOLEEON

airmail paper	hartee ahlilografeeas ah-ehroporiko
ballpoint	steelo
book	veevleeo
dictionary	leksikon
envelope	fahkelos
guidebook	odheegos (veevleeo)
ink	mel-la-nee
magazine	periodhiko
map	hartees
road map	odhigos hartees
a map of Greece (Athens)	ena hartee tees Elladhas (Ahtheenas)
newspaper	efimehreedha
in English	st'anglika
notebook	tetradhio
novels in English	meethistoreemata st'anglika
(sheet of) paper	meea kola hartee
pen	steelo
pencil	moleevee
postcard	kart-postahl
scissors	psaleedhee
writing paper	hartee ahlilografeeas
Do you have any foreign publications?	Eh-hee kseness ekdhosess?

PHOTOGRAPHY — FOTOGRAFEEA

How much is it to process this film?	Poso kahnee ya na toh emfaneeseteh aftoh?
How much for each print?	Poso ya katheh kopia?
One (two) copies of each.	Meea kopia (dheeo kopiess) ahpo kath'ena.
When will it be ready?	Poteh tha eenay ehtimo?
I'd like a film for this camera.	Thelo feelm ya aftee tee mee-hanee
B&W (film)	ahspromavro
camera	fotografikee mee-hanee
color (film)	eng-hromo
film	feelm
for prints	ya kopiess
for slides	ya slaeeds
flash	flahs
lens	fahkos
light meter	fotohmetro

SMOKING

Cigarettes are generally sold only in kiosks (peh**reep**tera) although on the smaller islands and in villages you may occasionally see them in tavernas, cafés and grocery stores. **Most kiosks close fairly early, so stock up if you plan to stay out late.** Greece grows and exports a lot of tobacco, so smoking is a very respected activity in the country and rarely banned anywhere. American and European are widely available but more expensive. Greek cigarettes are excellent and run the gamut from pungent to very light.

A packet of cigarettes, please.	ena paketto tsigara, parakalo.
Are these cigarettes strong/mild?	Afta ta tsigara eenoon dheenata/elafra?
Do you have a light?	Eh-heteh fohs?
Do you have any American	Eh-hee Amerikanika tsigara?

cigarettes?

cigar	pooro
cigarette papers	tsigaroharta
cigarettes	tsigara
a carton of cigarettes	ena hartohnee tsigara
filtered	meh feeltra
filterless	horees feeltro
flint	pehtra
lighter fluid	venzeenee ya ahnapteera
lighter	ahnapteera
matches	speerta
menthol	mentholee
pipe	tseemboukee
tobacco	kahpnos

ELECTRICAL APPLIANCES EELEKTRIKA EEDHEE

adapter	prosarmostees
battery	bah-tahreea
cd player	seedee
fan	ahnemisteeras
hairdryer	seswahr *or* peestolaki
heating coil	peeneeo
iron (for clothing)	seedhero
plug	preeza
portable tv	foreetee
radio	rah-dheeoh-fono
record (*noun*)	dheeskos
tape (cassette)	kasetta
tape recorder	kasetoh-fono
television	teeliorasi
transformer	meta-heematistee

video (player)	veesee-**ahr** *or* vee-deeo-kase**toh**-fono
videotape	vee-deeo-ka**set**ta

SIZE — **MEG**ATHOS

small	mee**kro**
big	me**ga**lo
heavy	va**ree**
light	ela**fro**
more	pee**oo** po**lee**
less	lee**go**tero
smaller	mee**kro**tero
too much/many	**pa**ra po**hlee**/**poh**la
many	**poh**la
enough	ar**ke**toh
that's enough	**ee**nay ar**ke**toh
also	ee**pee**sees
a little bit	**lee**go

11. WHAT'S TO SEE

In virtually every part of Greece, there are standard things to see, most of them beautiful, many of them breathtaking. The natural landscape has every possible variety, from the snow-covered mountains of the north to the equally snow-covered mountains of the country's southern-most point, the island of Crete. There are incredibly beautiful gorges all over the country, as well as fabulous beaches, and stunning architecture as well as archeological sites that come not just from the classical period but the Byzantine and Ottoman eras as well. It is not too much of an exaggeration to say that in almost every town and on very island, there is a museum worth visiting and a sight (and/or site) worth seeing.

Do you have a guidebook/local map?	Eh-hee enas ohdheegos/topikos hartees?
Is there a guide who speaks English?	Eeparhee enas ohdheegos poo Meelaee Anglika?
What are the main attractions?	Peeah eenoun ee keeriess ahksiotheh-ata?
What is that?	Tee eenay aftoh?
How old is it?	Poso hronon eenay?
May I take a photograph?	Boroh na vgalo meea fotografeea?
What time does it open/close?	Tee ora ahneeghee/kleenee?
Is there an entrance fee?	Eh-hee timee eeso-dhou?
How much?	Poso?
Are there any night clubs?	Eh-hee kabareh?
Where can I hear local folk music?	Poo boroh na ahkooso topikee dheemotikee moosikee?
How much does it cost to get in?	Poso kosteezi na boh?
What is there to do in evenings?	Tee eepar-hee na kahnomeh ta the vradhia?
Is there a concert?	Eh-hee seenavlee-a?

When is the wedding?	Poteh eenay oh **gah**mos?
What time does it begin?	Tee **ora** ar**hee**zee?
Can we swim here?	Bo**roo**may na **pah**meh ko**leem**bee **edho**?

dancing	ho**ros**
disco	**dees**ko
disk-jockey	deesk**j**okee
exhibition	**ek**thesee
folk dancing	laee**kos** horos
folk music	dheemo**ti**kee moosi**kee**
jazz	tzahz
party	**glen**dee
rock'n'roll	**roken**rol
blues	ta blooz

BUILDINGS	K**TEE**RIA
academy	ah-ka-dhee-**meea**
apartment	dhee-ah-**mer**isma
archaeological	arhay-ologhi**koh**
art gallery	peenako**thee**kee
bakery	**for**nos
bar	bahr
apartment block	polee-ka-ti**kee**a
building	**kteer**io
casino	ka**see**no
castle	ka**stel**lo *or* for**tet**za
cemetery	nekro**pol**eeo
church	ek**lee**seea
cinema	see**nema**
city-map	**har**tee tees po**lees**
college	kole**ghee**o
concert hall	oh**dhee**on
concert	seenav**lee**a

elevator	ahsan**sehr**
embassy	prezveea
hospital	nosoko**mee**o
house	**spee**tee
library	veevliot**hee**kee
main square	kentri**kee** plat**ee**a
market	ahgo**ra**
monastery	mohnas**tee**ri
monument	mnee**mee**o
mosque	tza**mee**
museum	moo**see**o
nightclub	kaba**reh**
old city	pah**lioh** po**lees**
opera house	**oh**pera *or* leeri**kee** ski**nee**
park	**par**ko
parliament building	ee vou**lee**
restaurant	estiatorion
ruins	arhay-**oh**-titess
shop	maga**zee** *or* **ka**tastima
school	sko**lee**o
shrine	ee-**eh**ros **to**pos
stadium	stad**hee**o
statue	**ah**galma
synagogue	seenago**gyee**
temple	na**ohs**
theatre	**theh**-atro
tomb	**tah**fos
tower	**peer**gos
university	panepis**tee**mio
zoo	zo-olog-**yi**kos **kee**pos

OCCASIONS

birth	**yen**isee
death	**than**atos

funeral	keedheea
marrlage	**gah**mos

RELIGIOUS HERITAGE

The Greek Orthodox Church is one of a number of Orthodox churches which broke away from the Roman Catholic church in 1054. The single basic difference between the Catholic and Orthodox churches is the latter's refusal to accept papal authority, while the Orthodox churches differ from Protestant ones in embracing many distinctly Catholic beliefs and practices, such as the intrinsic grace of the Sacrament and a veneration of the Virgin Mary. Finally, there is a touch of both Protestantism and Catholicism in the fact that although Orthodox parish priests are permitted to marry, the upper ranks of the clergy and its monks are not.

Apart from its religious function, the church is very much of a social and political force in Greece, and its bishops are constantly embroiling themselves in affairs which other countries have long ago decided should be left to the state. On the other hand, the parish priests are, for the most part, eminently non-authoritarian; often married and with children, they tend to share not only their community's manual labor but also a bit of its members' moral lapses; were it not for their beards and cassocks, it would sometimes be extremely difficult to tell the priests from their congregations and, occasionally, its sinners.

Holidays & festivals -- Inasmuch as every day of the year is a Saint's Day, it is virtually impossible to have a secular holiday without some religious connotations.

Secular holidays -- There are only three truly secular holidays throughout the year and one of them - **March 25th, Greek Independence Day** - is also the date of the Annunciation to the Virgin Mary, an extremely important religious event, so the two celebrations have become almost indistinguishable from one another. The other two public holidays are May 1st, the **Greek Labor Day** as well as the Spring Festival, and **October 28th**, which commemorates the day in World War II said "No" (Oh-hee) to Mussolini's request for "passage" through Greece. **Carnival** is also theoretically a secular event but since it is so inextricably bound to the coming of Lent, it cannot help having enormous religious overtones.

Religious festivals occur on major Saint's Days, usually at or around the church named after the saint, or in villages or areas for which a particular saint has some special significance. On the preceding evening, there is much dancing, drinking and feasting, often completely or partially free of charge.

The most important national religious festivals in Greece are, in order of the liturgical calendar: January 1 (**St. Basil**), January 6 (**Epiphany**), **Easter Sunday** (a movable feast which must fall after both the Jewish Passover and the first full moon after the first day of spring), May 21 (**Sts. Constantine and Helen**), and August 15 (**Assumption**). **Christmas** has nowhere near the importance of Easter, with presents being traditionally given on the feast of St. Basil, who is the Greek Santa Claus.

Name Days — It is a person's Name Day rather than his birthday which is celebrated in Greece. This is because the given name of a child carries with it such a wealth of family, religious, and historical connotations that the date on which the baby is born pales by comparison. Greeks having the name of a saint celebrate on the day of that saint and those with historical or mythological names not included on the Orthodox calendar celebrate on All Saints' Day, which falls on the eighth Sunday after Easter.

12. FINANCE

Currency - This is the Greek drachma, which has been named as such since Classical times. It has been relatively stable in recent years but the Greek economy is in such a potentially precarious state that nothing is certain. Changing money anywhere but at a bank is entirely against the law, and since there is not much to be gained by it anyway, you should do it only when you've run out of Greek money and need to pay for something on the spot, say in a restaurant.

In banks, passports are needed for all foreign exchange transactions. Keep the slips they give you afterwards as they will be vital should you wish to exchange your Greek money back into foreign currency before you leave. These proofs of your having had foreign currency to exchange are also important if you want to renew your visa for a longer stay.

I want to change some dollars.	Thelo na alahkso dholaria.
I want to change some pounds.	Thelo na alahkso leeress.
Where can I change some money?	Poo boroh na alahkso hreemata?
What is the exchange rate?	Tee eenay toh seenalagma?

dollar	dholaree
franc	frahnko
mark	marko
pound	leera

bank notes	hartonomeesmata
calculator	ahrithmo-mee-hanee
cashier	tahmeeas
coins	kehrmata
credit card	peestotikee karta
commission	promeethia
exchange	seenalagma
loose change	pseela
signature	eepografee

SOCIAL ORGANIZATION

It can safely be said that the Greeks' attitude towards society can be summed up as follows: Governments may change but the family (and sometimes the Church) are forever. Through thick and thin, it is and always has been the family unit which has nurtured, supported and saved both the individual and the country. In a way, this concept is a reflection of Greece's geography - the family being an island of stability in a very unpredictable sea - and may have been to a good degree formed by it. Throughout the ages there has been as much of a Greek diaspora as there has been a Jewish one, and it is significant that both social organization have had strong family units as well as a strong religious structure.

While the clergy of the Greek Orthodox Church may have at times been excessively political, they have nevertheless been vital in keeping the Greeks' national identity intact in spite of almost two millennium of foreign domination and were, particularly after the destruction of the library at Alexandria, virtually the only repository of its ancient, "pagan" heritage. It was certainly no coincidence that in 1821, at a monastery in the northern Peloponnese, the man who raised the flag of revolt against the Turks was an archbishop.

13. COMMUNICATIONS

Telecommunications -- OTE (written in blue letters on silver metallic signs as OTE and pronounced oh**teh**) is the logogram of the Telecommunications Organization of Greece, which handles both **telegrams** and **telephone calls**. OTE offices are theoretically open 24 hours a day, but this is true only in the larger cities and towns; on islands, they tend to close both at night and during the afternoon siesta hours. In Athens, the main OTE office is quite near Constitution Square, two blocks down Stadiou St.

An automatic dialing system for foreign and domestic calls has now been established virtually throughout Greece. One can telephone from either the OTE officeor from any sidewalk kiosk, café, hotel, restaurant, or shop which has an automatic counter (rol**loee**) hooked up to the telephone. One pays in terms of the number of units (mon**a**dhess) that have been marked up on the counter during the call. The automatic area codes for all countries and major cities within the system as well as interantional dailing codes can be found in the front pages of all telephone directories. Collect calls must be made from the OTE office.

Post office -- Greek post offices are open Mon - Fri, although the hours differ from city to town and island to island. All are definitely open in the mornings from about 8 a.m. to noon. Afternoon hours depend on the local customs and shopping hours.

Postage stamps can be bought either at the post office or at certain sidewalk kiosks, although the owners may not necessarily know the rates for various countries.

Post Restante (written that way on envelopes) is the general address to which all your mail can be sent, i.e. Your Name, Poste Restante, Patmos, Greece. When asking for mail, you must present your passport as identification. Packages and registered letters must be left open for inspection before they are sent abroad.

During the tourist seasons it often takes a month or more for letters to reach and arrive from foreign shores.

AT THE POST OFFICE

post office, the   toh taheedhrom**ee**o
   (written on yellow signs with black letters as:
   ΤΑΧΥΔΡΟΜΕΙΟΝ or ΕΛΤΑ)

Where is the post office?	Poo **eenay** toh taheedhro**mee**o?
What time does the post office open?	Tee **o**ra ah**nee**yee toh taheedhro**mee**o?
What time does the post office close?	Tee **o**ra **klee**nee toh taheedhro**mee**o?
Where is the mail box?	Poo **eenay** toh gramatokee**vo**tio?
Is there any mail for me?	**Eh**-hee **gra**mata ya **me**na?
How long will it take to arrive?	**Po**sess **mehr**ess the**lee** na **ftah**si?
How much does it cost to send this to...?	**Po**so **kah**nee ya na toh **stee**lo stee...?
I would like some stamps.	Tha**ee**thela gramatoh**see**ma.
I would like to send ...	Tha**ee**thela na toh **stee**lo....
a letter	**e**na **gra**mma.
a postcard	**e**na kartpos**tahl**
a parcel	**e**na **dhe**ma

address, the	ee dhee-**ef**theensee
return address	oh ahpost**leh**-efs
aerogram	ah-ehro**grah**ma
airmail	ah-ehropori**koh**
care of (c/o)	meh**reem**nee tou
express	eks**press**
general delivery	pohst res**tahnt**
letter, a	**e**na **grah**ma (pl. **grah**mata)
money order	epita**gyee**
package, a	**e**na **dheh**ma
postage, the	ta takhee**dhro**mika
post card	kartpos**tahl**
printed matter	en**tee**pa
registered	seesti**me**no

213

special delivery	ekspress
stamp, a	**ena** gra**matoh**simo (pl. gra**matoh**sima)
(collection	seelo**gyee**)
surface mail	**tak**tikoh takhee**dhro**meeo

TELEPHONING, TELEGRAPHING

telephone, a	**ena** teele**h**fono
telegram, a	**ena** teeleh**gra**feema
directory	kah**tah**logos
Is there a telephone?	**Eh**-hee teele**h**fono?
I want to send a telegram to...	**Thel**o na **stee**lo teeleh**gra**feema stee...
I want to telephone to...	**Thel**o na teelefo**nee**so stee...
The number is...	Oh ahrith**mos ee**nay...
long distance	eeperas**ti**koh
automatic	ahf-**toh**matoh
collect	kolekt
busy	voo**ee**zee ("*buzzing*") or mee**laee** ("*talking*")
doesn't answer	dhen ah**pan**daee
wrong number	**lah**thos
I couldn't (can't) hear	dhen bo**roo**sa (bo**roh**) n'ah**koo**so.
Where is the telephone?	Poo **ee**nay toh teele**h**fono?
May I use your phone?	Bo**roh** na hreesimope-**oo**so toh **dhee**ko sahs teele**h**fono?
Can I telephone from here?	Bo**roh** na teeleh**fo**neeso ah**po** eh-**dho**?
Can you help me get this number?	Bo**ree**teh na meh vo-ee**thee**seteh na **pah**ro aftoh toh ah**ree**thmo?
I would like to make a	Tha-**ee**thela na teeleh**fo**neeso.

phone call.	
I would like to send a fax.	Tha-eethela na **steelo ena** fahks.
I would like to send a telex.	Tha-**ee**thela na **steelo ena** teleks.
I would like to send a telegram.	Tha-**ee**thela na **steelo ena** teeleh**grah**feema.
What is the code for...?	Tee **ee**nay toh ah**f**tomatoh ya teen....
What is the international code?	Tee **ee**nay oh dhee-ethnos kodhikos?
The number is...	Oh ahreethmos eenay...
The extension is...	Oh esotehrikos eenay...
It's busy.	Meelaee.
I've been cut off.	Mou **k**optikeh ee gram**mee**.
Can you help me get this number?	Bor**ee**teh na meh vo-ee**thee**seteh na **pah**ro af**toh** toh ahreethmo?
Can I dial direct?	Bor**oh** na teelehfon**ee**so kat'ef**thee**ahn?
Where is the nearest phone?	Poo **ee**nay toh kondinoteero teeleh**f**ono?
I would like to speak to...	Tha-**ee**thela na meel**ee**so meh...
Can I leave a message?	Bor**oh** na ah**f**eeso **mee**nima?
fax	fahks
e-mail	**ee**-mail
international operator	dhee-eth**nees** teelehfononi**tees**
Internet	**ee**nternet
modem	**mo**dem
operator	teelehfononi**tees**

mobile phone	foree**toh** teele**h**fono
telex	**tel**eks

14. THE OFFICE

chair	karekla
computer	eelektonikos eepologhistees
desk	grahfeeo
drawer	seertahree
fax	fahks
file	fakelos
meeting	seenahndisi
paper	hartee
pen	steelo
pencil	moleevee
photocopier	fotoandee-tipikee meehanee
printer	ekteepotees
report	ahnafora *or* ekthesi
ruler	harakas
telephone	teelehfono
telex	teleks
typewriter	grahfomeehanee

15. THE CONFERENCE

a break for refreshments	dheeahlima ya ahnapsitika
conference room	ethousa ya dhee-**ah**-skepsi
copy	an**dee**grahfo
discussion	seez**ee**tisi
guest speaker	proskekli**men**os omeeli**tees**
a paper	anak**ee**nosi
podium	ek**seh**dhra
projector	provol**eh**-efs
speaker	omeeli**tees**
subject	**thema**

16. ANIMALS

MAMMALS

bear	arkoudha
bull	tavros
cat	gata
cow	ah-yeladha
deer	elafee
dog	skeelos
donkey	ga-eedharos *or* ga-eedhooree
flock	kopadhee
goat	katzeekee
herd	ah-yelee
horse	ahlogo
lamb	arnee
mouse	pondheekee
mule	moolaree
pig	goroonee
rabbit	koonelee
ram	kreeahree
rat	ahrooray-os
sheep	provato
wolf	leekos

BIRDS

bird	poolee
chicken/hen	kotohpoulo/kota
rooster	petinos
crow	kourouna
duck	papeea
eagle	ah-ehtos
goose	heena

owl	kookoovahya
turkey	galopoulo

INSECTS AND AMPHIBIANS

ant	meermeeghee
bee	melissa
butterfly	petaloudha
caterpillar	kambia
cockroach	kahtsareedha
fish	psahree
fleas	pseelos
fleas	pseelee
fly	meega
frog	vatra-hos
insect	endomo
lizard	sahvra
louse	pseera
mosquito	kounoupee
snail	sahlingaree
snake	feedhee
spider	ahrahnee
termite	tehrmeetees
viper	oh-heeah
wasp	sfeeka
worm	skooleekee

17. COUNTRYSIDE

canal	kahnahlee
cave	speelayo
earthquake	seesmos
fire	fotiah
foothills	propo-dhess
footpath	monopahtee
forest	dhasos
gorge	fahrahngee
hill	lofos
lake	leemnee
landslide	kahtoleestheesi
mountain	voono
mountain pass	dheeodhos
peak	korifee
plain	kambos
plant	feetoh
ravine	fahrahngee
river	potahmee
rock	vrahos
stream	potamahki
summit	korifee
tree	dhentro
valley	keeladha
waterfall	kahtarahktees
a wood	dhasos

18. THE WEATHER

In summer, it is hot (75-100° F.), and, until the mid-1980's, was virtually cloudless and rainless. There is some humidity, particularly in the larger cities and certain, but not all islands. The prevailing summer wind, called the meltemee, comes from the north and is a blessing; on Crete, where there is also a southern wind which occasionally sweeps in from the Sahara and turns the island into an oven.

In winter, the weather varies considerably. In the north and mountains, there is snow; while south of Athens, in the plains, the temperature rarely drops below freezing. The temperature averages about 55° and occasionally soars into the 70's. Rain falls, but not as constantly as most foreigners think when they refer to Greece's "rainy season". It is not monsoon time, and there are quite a few days that are as cloudless and beautiful as summer. The prevailing winds are from all directions, but the Greeks say that the worst weather comes from Italy.

In the spring and fall, the weather is superlative, ranging in temperature from 65° to 85° F. Occasionally, there are some massive rainstorms. The winds vary in strength and direction and are often fierce enough to stop all travel by ship, often for days.

What's the weather like?	Tee **kah**nee oh kay**ros**?
The weather is ...today.	Oh kay**ros kah**nee....**seemehra.**
cold	**kree**oh
cool/fresh	dhros**eroh**
freezing	pahg-**yehro**
hot	**zes**tee
very hot	po**lee zes**tee
windy	ahnemo**dhees**
rainy	vro**heros**
It is...	**Eh**-hee
misty	**poo**see
cloudy	seene**fiah**
foggy	o**meehk**lee
It is raining.	**Vreh**ee.
It is snowing.	Hioh**neezi**

It is sunny.	Eh-hee leeakadha.
cloud	seenefa
fog	omeehlee
frost	pahgoniah
full moon	pahnselinos
heatwave	keema kavsonos
ice	pagos
midsummer	kardhiah tou kalokerioo
midwinter	toh kahtaheemono
mild winter	malakos heemonas
moon	fengahree
rain	vrohee
severe winter	varees heemonas
sleet	heeono-nehro
snow	heeohnee
solstice	eeliostasio
star	ahstehree
sun	eelios
sunny	leeakadha
thaw	leeohsimo
weather, the	oh kayros
wind	ahnemos

SEASONS

spring	ahneeksi
summer	kalokayree
autumn	ftheenoporo
winter	heemonahs

19. CAMPING

Where can we camp?	Poo bor**oo**meh na **kah**noomeh **kamp**ing?
Can we camp here?	Bor**oo**meh na **kah**noomeh **kamp**ing ehdh**oh**?
Is it safe to camp here?	**Ee**nay ahs-fal**ess** na **kah**noomeh **kamp**ing ehdh**oh**?
Is there drinking water?	**Eh**-hee p**o**simo n**e**hro?
May we light a fire?	Ehpee**trep**eteh na ahn**ap**soomeh fot**iah**?

axe	tsek**oo**ree
backpack	sak**ee**dhio
bucket	k**oo**vahs
campsite	katask**ee**nosee
can opener	ahnit**ee**ri konseh**rv**as
compass	peeks**ee**dha
firewood	kavso-ks**ee**la
flashlight	fah**kos**
gas canister	fee**ah**lee **gah**zee
hammer	sf**eh**ree
lamp	**lah**mpa
mattress	**stro**ma
penknife	soog-yadh**ak**ee
rope	sk**ee**nee
sleeping bag	sleeping bag
stove	**so**mba
tent	sk**ee**nee
tent pegs	**ah**salos ya sk**ee**nee
water bottle	fee**ah**lee n**eh**roo

20. IN CASE OF EMERGENCY

Complaining - All major complaints should be reported to the local Tourist Police. They take their jobs very seriously and will come down hard on any of their countrymen whom they suspect of having done something to tarnish the reputations of Greece among foreigners. Minor complaints can thus be handled by simply <u>threatening</u> to go to the police, because if anyone has in reality cheated you, they will quickly make things right to avoid this. Interestingly, most Greeks will advise you not to trust Greeks – excepting of course themselves. In general, there is a grain of truth in this, but no more than elsewhere.

Crime - The Greeks pride themselves on the low rate of crime in their country, and until recently it was not unusual to see convertibles parked on the street with the top down and cassettes strewn safely on the seat. With, however, the influx into the country not only of more and more hard drugs but of often desperate refugees from Albania and other formerly Communist countries, the crime rate has risen sharply. This includes not only theft but murder and rape. The general rule is to be careful in the larger cities of Athens, Thessaloniki and Piraeus and in the countryside bordering the Balkans. Elsewhere, the same relatively idyllic state that existed a decade ago still persists; and if there is a crime, you will find that the perpetrator is most often not Greek but a foreigner.

Disabled facilities - These are almost non-existent in the country with the exception perhaps of a few enlightened tourist hotels.

Toilet - Public facilities are few and hard to find. Often they are underground at the main squares of a city or town. Because of the country's chronic summertime water shortage, most restaurants and hotels zealously reserve their toilets for certified customers, closing them with keys otherwise. Also, as most toilets have no toilet paper, it is advisable to always carry a packet of tissues with you, if not a roll.

Help!	Vo**ee**thia!
Could you help me please?	Bor**ee**teh na meh voee**thee**teh, sahs paraka**lo?**
Do you have a telephone?	**Eh**-hee teel**eh**fono?
Can I use your telephone?	Bor**oh** na hreesimopee-**oo**so toh teel**eh**fono sahs?
Where is the nearest telephone?	Poo **ee**nay toh kondi**no**tero teel**eh**fono?

Does the phone work?	Toh teelehfono leetourg-yee?
Get help quickly!	Kalehsteh voeethia ahmehsos!
Call the police!	Teelehfoneesteh steen astinomeea!
I'll call the police!	Tha teelehfoneeso steen stinomeea.
Is there a doctor near here?	Eh-hee yatros konda?
Call a doctor.	Teelehfoneesteh yiatro.
Call an ambulance.	Teelehfoneesteh ahsthenoforo.
It's an emergency!	Eenay ahnanghee!
I'm sick. (male/female)	Eemay ahrostos/ ahrostee.
I'm not feeling well.	Dhen aysthahnomay kahlah.
I ate....	Efagah...
I drank...	Eepia...
I took...	Peerah...
It hurts (here).	Pohnaee (ehdho).
Where is the doctor?	Poo eenay oh yatros?
Where is the doctor's office (clinic/hospital)?	Poo eenay toh yatreeoh (tee klinikee/ toh nosokomee-oh)?
Where is the pharmacy?	Poo eenay toh farmakeeo?
Where is the dentist?	Poo eenay toh odhondee-atros?
Where is the police station?	Poo eenay toh ahstinomikoh tmeema?
There's been an accident!	Egyeeneh ena dheesteeheema.
Is anyone hurt?	Pleeg-yeethikeh kahnees?
This person (m./f.) is hurt.	Ahftos/ Ahftee pleeg-yeethikeh.
There are people injured.	Eeparhee ahnthropee pleeg-yeethikav.
Don't move!	Mee kooniesteh!

Go away!	**Fee**geteh!
I am lost.	**Eh**-ho hathee.
I am ill (male/female).	**Ee**may **ah**rostos/ **ah**rostee.
I've been raped.	**Ka**pios meh **vee**aseh.
Take me to a doctor.	**Pan**teh meh s'**e**na yia**tro**.
I've been robbed!	Meh **klep**saneh!
Thief!	**Klef**tees!
My... has been stolen.	Meh **klep**saneh...
I have lost my...	E**ha**sa...
my bags	tees va**leet**sess mou
my camera	teen fotografi**kee** meeha**nee** mou
my handbag	teen **tsahn**da mou
my laptop computer	toh laptop mou
my money	ta hree**ma**ta mou
my passport	toh dheeava**tee**rioh mou
my travelers' checks	ta traveler's tzeks mou
my wallet	toh porto**fo**li mou
My possessions are insured.	Ta prag**ma**ta mou **ee**neh ahsfalis**me**na.
I have a problem.	**Eh**-ho pro**vel**ma.
I didn't do it.	Dhen to **e**kana.
I'm sorry.	Seeg**no**mee.
I apologize.	Meh seekho**ree**teh.
I didn't realize anything was wrong.	Dhen kata**la**va pohs ee**pir**heh pro**vlee**ma.
I want to contact my embassy.	**The**lo na mee**lee**so meh teen prez**vee**ah mou.
I want to contact my consulate.	**The**lo na mee**lee**so meh toh prokse**nee**oh mou.

I speak English.	Meelaoh Ahnglika.
I need an interpreter.	**Thelo enas dhee-ermineeahs**
Where are the toilets?	Poo eenay ee too-ahlettess? |ульт

clinic — kleenikee
doctor — yiatros
nurse — nosokoma
hospital — nosokomeeoh
policeman — ahstinomos
police — ahstinomeea
police station — ahstinomikoh tmeema

21. HEALTHCARE

Health/medical information - Greece has free socialized medical care, but often the hospitals where it is available are extremely crowded and understaffed. The private clinics in major cities are generally excellent: clean, well-staffed and having the most modern equipment available. Some of them will take foreign medical insurance such as Blue Cross: others will not. No vaccinations are necessary for Greece although it may be wise to take such boosters as those for tetanus and various others usually recommended for trips to that area of the world. Pharmacies are well-stocked and there is, by law, at least one designated pharmacy always open 24 hours a day even on Sundays. Lists with the addresses of the open pharmacies are posted in the windows of the others.

What's the trouble?	Tee eenay toh provleema?
I am sick (male/female).	Eemay ahrostos/ahrostee.
My friend (male/female) is sick.	Oh feelos/ee feelee mou eenay ahrostos/ahrostee.
May I see a female doctor?	Boroh na dhoh meea yiatros?
I have medical insurance.	Eh-ho ahsfalia eegyeeahs.

AILMENTS

I'm not feeling well.	Dhen aysthanomay kahla.
It hurts here.	Ponaee eh-dho.
I have been vomiting.	Ehkana emetoh.
I feel dizzy.	Zaleesomay.
I can't eat.	Dhen boroh na fao.
I can't sleep.	Dhen boroh na keemitho.
I feel worse.	Aysthanomay heerotera.
I feel better.	Aysthanomay kaleetera.
I am...	Eemay...
Are you ...?	Eesteh...
diabetic	dheeahveetikos
epileptic	epileeptikos
asthmatic	ahs-thmatikos

I'm pregnant.	Eemay **eng**-eeohs.
I have...	**Eh**-ho...
You have...	**Eh**-heteh...
a temperature	peeretoh
an allergy	ah-lehr-**ghee**a
an infection	moleensi
an itch	**mee**a fagoora
fever	peeretoh
I have a cold.	**Eh**-ho kree-oh-**lo**-yima.
I have a cough.	**Eh**-ho **vee**ha.
I have a headache.	**Eh**-ho ponokefalo.
I have toothache.	**Eh**-ho ponodondos.
I have a sore throat.	**Eh**-ho ponolaymos.
I have a stomachache.	**Eh**-ho stomahoponos.
I have a fever.	**Eh**-ho peeretoh.
I have backache.	Po**nae**e ee **plah**tee mou.
I have constipation.	**Eh**-ho dhees-kee-**lioh**tees.
I have diarrhea.	**Eh**-ho dhee**ah**ria.
I have a heart condition.	**Eh**-ho teen kar-**dhiah** mou.
I have a pain in my heart.	Po**nae**e stee kar-**dhee**ah mou.

MEDICATION

I take this medication.	**Peh**rno af**toh** toh far**ma**ko.
I need medication for...	**The**lo far**ma**ko ya...
What type of medication is this?	Tee **ee**-dhos far**ma**ko **Ee**nay ah**ftoh**?
How many times a day must I take it?	Posess for**ess** teen ee**meh**ra **pre**pee na toh **pah**ro?
When should I stop?	**Po**teh **pre**pee na stama**tee**so?

I'm on antibiotics.	**Peh**rno andivee-ohti**ka**.
I'm allergic to ...	Eemay ah-lehr-ghi**kos**...
antibiotics	sta ahn-dee-vioti**ka**.
penicillin	steen penikil**ee**nee.
I have been vaccinated.	**Eh**-ho ka**nee** emvolio.
I have my own syringe.	**Eh**-ho teen **dhee**kee mou **see**ringa.
Is it possible for me to travel?	**Bo**roh na taksi**dhe**pso?

painkiller	ah-nal-**yee**tikos
tranquillizer	eeremisti**ko** **far**mako
aspirin	ahspi**ree**nee
antibiotic	ahn-dee-vioti**ko**
drug	**far**mako

HEALTH WORDS

AIDS	Ayds
alcoholic	alco-oli**kos**
alcoholism	alco-olis**mos**
anemia	ahnay**mee**a
amputation	ahkroteerias**mos**
anesthetic	ah-nays-thee**ti**ko
anesthetist	ah-nays-theesio**lo**gos
antibiotic	ahn-dee-vioti**ko**
antiseptic	ahn-dee-seepti**ko**
blood	**ay**ma
blood group	**oh**mas **ay**matos
blood pressure:	**pee**-esees **ay**matos
low blood pressure	epo**ta**si
high blood pressure	epehr-**ta**si
blood transfusion	me**tah**n-**yee**sees **ay**matos
bone	**ko**kalo
cancer	ka**kee**nos
cholera	ho**leh**ra

clinic	kleeni**kee**
dentist	oh-dhon-**dhee**-yatros
epidemic	epi-dhee-**mee**a
fever	peeretoh
flu	**gree**pee
fracture	**kah**tagma
germs	meekrovia
heart attack	**em**fragma
hepatitis	eepa**tee**tees
hygiene	ee-yee-**ee**nee
indigestion	dhees-**pep**seea
infection	mo**lee**nsi
influenza	**gree**pee
limb	**ah**kro
needle	velonee
nurse	noso**ko**ma
operation	eng**hee**risees
oxygen	ok**si**gono
pain	**po**nos
physiotherapy	feesiothera**pee**a
pins and needles	mou-dhee-**ah**-zo
rabies	**lee**sa
snake bite	**dha**-goma fee-dhee-**oo**
stethoscope	steetho**sko**pio
stomachache	stoma**ho**ponos
surgeon	heero**lo**gos
(act of) surgery	eng**hee**risees
syringe	see**rin**ga
thermometer	thehr-**mo**metro
toothache	pono-dhon-dos

EYESIGHT

I have broken my glasses.	**Eh**-ho spasi ta yaliah mou.
Can you repair them?	Bo**ree**teh na ta episke**va**seteh?

I need new lenses.	**Thelo** kay**no**rioos fah**koos**.
When can I collect them?	**Po**teh tha bo**res**so na toos **pah**ro?
How much do I owe you?	**Po**so sahs hros**ta**oh?
contact lenses	fah**kos** ehpa**feess**
contact lens solution	ee**gro** ya tous fah**kous** ehpa**feess**

22. TOOLS

binoculars	kee**ah**lia
brush	**voor**tsa
butane canister	feeahlee **gah**zi
cable	**ca**lo-dheeo
drill	treepa**nee**
glasses, sunglasses	yal**iah** too **ee**lio
hammer	sfee**ree**
handle	**heh**ree
hose	las**ti**ko *or* so**lee**nas
insecticide	endo-mok-**toh**-no
ladder	**ska**la
machine	mee-**ha**nee
microscope	meekro**sko**pio
nail	**pro**-ha
padlock	loo**ket**ta
paint	boo-**ya**
plank	sah**nee**-dhee
plastic	plas**ti**ko
rope	skee**nee**
rubber	las**ti**ko *or* ka-oot**souk**
rust	skoo**riah**
saw	pree**oh**nee
scissors	psa**lee**-dhee
screw	**vee**-dha
screwdriver	katsa**vee**-dha
spade	ftee-**ah**ree
spanner	klee-**dhee**
string	**spahn**-gos
stove	**som**ba
telescope	teeleh**sko**pio
varnish	vehr**nee**kee

23. THE CAR

Customs - When you enter the country, the car will be stamped into your passport and you will be given a limited "free use" permit, usually four months. This can be renewed up to a period of one year at the nearest customs authority, but the process sometimes (although not always; it depends on the mood of the local customs official) involves having a third party, a Greek, guaranteeing that he will pay all the duties and taxes should your car "disappear," i.e. be sold. Normally you will not be allowed to leave the country without your car and, since it is stamped in your passport, this is virtually impossible. However, in extenuating circumstances -- if, for instance, you should suddenly have to fly home because of an emergency -- you can arrange with the customs authorities at the airport or elsewhere to store the car, often at an exorbitant fee, until you return.

Driving - An international Driving License is required for all foreigners driving in Greece (with the exception of those holding EC licenses). Green cards for international insurance are not compulsory, but it would be prudent to have one anyway. Greek traffic regulations are in accord with those used throughout Europe and America. Speed limits vary from 60-75 m.p.h., on roads and highways to 25-40 m.p.h. within city and town limits.

Where can I rent a car?	Poo boroh na eneekiahso ena aftokeenitoh?
How much is it per day?	Poso kahnee teen eemehra?
How much is it per week?	Poso kahnee teen ev-dho-ma-dha?
Can I park here?	Boroh na parkaro eh-dho?
Are we on the right road?	Eemastay sto sosto dhromo?
Where is the nearest filling station?	Poo eenay toh kondinotero venzeena-dhiko?
Fill the tank please.	Yemiseh toh depositoh, sahs parakalo.
normal/super/diesel	kanoniko/soopehr/deezel
Check the oil/tires/ battery, please.	Elengksteh toh lah-dhee/ta lahsteeha/ tee bahtehreea sahs parakalo?
I've broken down.	Ee-ha meea vlahvee.

English	Greek
I have a puncture.	Eh-ho treepeema.
I don't have gas.	Dhen eh-ho venzeenee.
Our car is stuck (in a ditch).	Toh aftokeenitoh mahs eh-hee koleesi (s'ena lako.)
There's something wrong with this car.	Eeparhee ena provleema meh ahftoh toh ahftokeenitoh.
We need a mechanic.	Hreeahzomasteh ena meehaniko.
Where is the nearest garage?	Poo eenay toh kondinotero garahz?
Can you tow us?	Boreeteh na mahs remoulkareteh?
There's been an accident.	Ehyeeneh ena dheestee-heema.
My car has been stolen.	Meh klepsaneh toh aftokeenitoh mou.
Call the police.	Telehfoneesteh steen ahstinomeea..
driver's license	dheeploma
insurance policy	ee ahsfalia

WORDS

accelerator	gahzee
accident	dhisteehima
air	ah-ehras
battery	bahtareea
(to charge)	na forteesee
blow-out	klatarisma
brake	frehno
bumper	profilakteer
carburetor	karbiratehr
clutch	ambra-yahz
driver	oh-dheegos
engine	meekhanee
exhaust (pipe)	eksahtmisi
fan (belt)	looree
gears	ta-heetitess

Green Card	prahsinee karta
horn	klakson
ignition	dhee-akoptee
indicator light	toh flahs
inner tube	sambrella
jack	greelos
jumper cable	alo-dheeo meh tsimbee-dhess
lights (head)	ta fanaria
(signal)	toh flahs
(tail)	ta peeso fota
mechanic	meehanikos
muffler	seelansieh
neutral gear	nekro seemeeo
oil	ladhee
(high-pressure)	valvoleenee
passenger	epivatees
petrol	venzeenee
pressure	pee-esis
pump	ahndleea
punctured	treepimeno
radiator	psee-yeeoh
repair (to)	na episkevahsi
reverse	ohpees-then
shock absorber	amortisehr
spare parts	andalaktika
spark plug	boozee
speed	takheetita
steering wheel	teemohnee
tire	lastikho
(pressure)	pee-esis sta lastikha
(spare)	rehserva
transmission	sahsmahn
trunk	port-bagahz

valve	valvee-dha
wheel	trohos
windshield	par-breez

24. BOATING & FISHING

Boating - Boats of varying types can be rented but only rarely without their owners. A marvelous way to spend the day is with one of the locals exploring the coastline and small beaches of the area you're in.

Fishing - Fishing in Greece is no longer what it used to be because of massive, unending pollution of the Mediterranean and the illegal but wanton use of dynamite by some fishermen. Using a speargun is prohibited if you are wearing any sort of underwater breathing apparatus.

boat, a (the)	**mee**a (ee) **var**ka
fishing boat	kae**ekee**
motor boat	venzee**na**katos
rowboat	**var**ka meh koupiah
sailboat	**var**ka meh pah**nee**
yacht	ko**tee**ro

BOATING TERMS

aft	**pee**so
anchor	**ahn**ghira
barometer	va**ro**metro
falling	**pef**tee
rising	ah**nehr**hetay
berth (dock)	apo**vra**thra
boom	**pee**kee
bow	plo**ree**
buoy	seema**dhoo**ra
cabin	ca**bee**na
Cast off!	**Lee**seh!
chart	har**tees**
charter, a	ena **nah**vloma
charter (to)	nah**vlo**no
crew	**plee**roma
current	**rev**ma
Customs	Telo**nee**oh
deck	katah**stro**ma

dinghy	varkahkee
engine	meekhanee
forward	brostah
harbour	limahnee
lifebelt/jacket/saver	toh soseevio
moor (to)	na ormeeso
motor (outboard)	eksolemvios kiniteer
net	dheektee
oar	koupee
pier (large)	leemahnee
(small)	molos
port	leemahnee
Port Authority	Limanarheeoh
port (side)	ahristerah
propeller	propella
rudder	teemohnee
sail	pahnee
starboard	dheksiah
stern	preemnee
storm	foortoona, thee-ela
tide	pahleeria
wave	keema (pl. keemata)
weather forecast	provlepsis kayroo
wind	ah-eh

FISHING TERMS

fish (to)	na psarevo
fishing	psahrema
I'd like to go fishing.	Tha eethela na pao ya psahrevma.
bait, fly	dholoma
fishing boat	psarovarka
fish hook	ahngheestree

fishing line	ar**mee**dhee
fisherman	psa**rahs**
fish net	**dheek**tee
fishing rod	kah**lah**mee
spear	ka**mah**kee
spear gun	psaron**too**feko
tackle	**see**nerga psari**kees**
weight	mo**lee**vee *or* va**reed**hee

25. COLORS

color	hroma
dark	skooro
light	ahneektoh
medium	metrio
black	mahvro
blue	bleh
brown	kafeh
green	prahsino
orange	portokahlee
pink	rodhino *or* roz
purple	veesinee
red	kokino
white	lefko *or* ahspro
yellow	keetrino

26. SPORTS

As you would imagine of people who practically enshrined athletics with the Olympic Games, Greeks are fanatics for all kinds of sports, particularly soccer and basketball. In both they have done very well in international competition, and have inter- and intra-city rivalries that match anything in the U.S. in their intensity. A number of fading and up-and-coming American basketball players have made their mark on the major teams from Athens and Thessaloniki and one or more could be playing there when you are.

athletics	athleetika
ball	ballo
basketball	bahsket
chess	skahkee
goal	gol
horseracing	koursess
horse-riding	eepaseea
match , a	ena mahts
soccer match	po-dhos-feriko mahts
pitch	yeepo-dho
skiing	skee
soccer	poh-**dhos**-fero
stadium	stadheeo
swimming	koleembee
team	omah-dha
tennis	tenees
Who won?	Peeohs kehr-dhiseh?

27. THE BODY

ankle	ahstrahgalos
arm	hehree
back, the	plahtee
beard	moosee
blood	ayma
bone	kokalo
bottom	peesinos
breast, chest	steethos
chin	pigoonee
ear	ahftee
ears	ahftiah
elbow	ahngonas
eye	mahtee
eyes	mahtiah
face	prosopo
finger	dhahktilo
fingers	dhahktila
foot	pohdhee
feet	podhia
genitals	yenitika organa
hair, a	meea treeha
hairs (on body)	treehess
hair (on head)	mahliah
hand	hehree
head	kefahlee
heart	kar-dhiah
intestines	ta entera
jaw	sahgonee
kidney	nehfro
kidneys	nehfra
knee	gonatoh

leg	**poh**-dhee
lip	**hee**los
lips	**hee**la
liver	seekotee
lung	**pnevmon**
lungs	pnevmoness
mouth	**stoma**
muscle	mees
neck	**sveh**rkos
nerve	nevro
nose	**mee**tee
rib	plevro
ribs	plevra
shoulder	**oh**mos
stomach	stoh**mah**kee
teeth	**dhon**-deea
throat	**laymos**
thumb	ahndeeheer
toe	**dahk**tilo po-dheeoo
tongue	**glosa**
tooth	**dhon**-dee
vein	**fleva**
veins	**flev**ess
womb	**mee**tra
wrist	**karpos**

28. TIME AND DATES

century	ayonas
decade	dheka-ehteea
year	hronos
month	meena
fortnight	dheka-pentheemeron
week	ev-dho-ma-dha
day (24 hour period)	mehra
hour	ora
minute	leptoh
second	dhef-tero-leptoh
dawn	ahvghee
sunrise	anatolee tou eeleeoo
morning	proee
day	mehra
noon	mesimehree
afternoon	ahpoy-evma
evening	vra-dhee
sunset	eelio-vaseelima
night	neekta
midnight	meesa-neekta
four days before	preen tehserees mehress
three days before	preen treess mehress
the day before yesterday	prokthess
yesterday	ekthess
last night	kthess vrah-dhee
today	seemehra
tomorrow	ahvrio
the day after tomorrow	meth'ahvrio
three days from now	mehta ahpo treess mehress

four days from now	mehta ahpo tehserees mehress
the year before last	preen **dhee**-o hronia
last year	**peh**risee
this year	eh**f**etos
next year	toh **hr**onoo
the year after next	mehta ahpo **dhee**-o hronia
last week	preen **meea** ev-dho-**mah**-dha
this week	af**tee** teen ev-dho-**mah**-dha
next week	teen **ahlee** ev-dho-**mah**-dha
this morning	af**toh** toh proee
now	torah
tonight	ah**pohp**see
yesterday morning	ek**thess** toh proee
yesterday afternoon	ek**thess** toh ah**poy**-evma
yesterday night	ek**thess** toh **vra**-dhee
tomorrow morning	**ah**vrio toh proee
tomorrow afternoon	**ah**vrio toh ah**poy**-evma
tomorrow night	**ah**vrio toh **vra**-dhee
in the morning	toh proee
in the afternoon	toh ah**poy**-evma
in the evening	toh **vra**-dhee
past	pahrel**thon**
present	pah**ron**
future	**mel**lon
What date is it today?	Tee ee-mero-mee**neea** eenay **see**mehra?
What time is it?	Tee **o**ra **ee**nay?
It is... o'clock.	**Ee**nay....ee **o**ra.

SEASONS
summer	kalo**keh**ree
autumn	ftheenoporo
wInter	heemonahs
spring	**ah**neeksee

DAYS OF THE WEEK
Monday	Dhef-**teh**ra
Tuesday	**Tree**tee
Wednesday	Te**tar**tee
Thursday	**Pemp**tee
Friday	Paraskevee
Saturday	**Sah**vatoh
Sunday	Kee-ree-ah**kee**

MONTHS
There two names, formal and informal, for each month. Below is the most commonly used, the informal.

January	Yenarees
February	Flevarees
March	**Mar**tees
April	Ah**pree**lees
May	**Ma**ees
June	**Yoo**nio
July	**Yoo**lio
August	Ahv**goo**stoh
September	Sep**tem**vrees
October	Ok**to**vrees
November	No**em**vrees
December	Dheh-**kem**vrees

29. NUMBERS AND AMOUNTS

The first number of each group of ten except ten (i.e. one, twenty, thirty, etc.) radically changes its form depending on the gender of the thing being counted, as indicated below. The other numbers change but not so radically. In general, one counts as in English.

0	meedhen
1	enas (m) meea (f) ena (n)
2	dheeoh
3	treeah
4	tehsera
5	pendeh
6	eksee
7	eftah *or* eptah
8	awktoh
9	enaya
10	dheka
11	en-dheka
12	dho-dheka
13	dheka-treeah
14	dheka-tehsera
15	dheka-pendeh
16	dheka-eksee
17	dheka-eftah
18	dheka-awktoh
19	dheka-enaya
20	eekosee
21	eekosee ena (meea) (enas)
22	eekosee dheeoh
30	treeahnda
40	sarahnda
50	peneenda
60	ekseenda

70	ev-dho**meen**da
80	awk-**dhon**-da
90	ene**neen**da
100	e**ka**toh
101	e**katon ena** (**meea**) (**enas**)
102	e**katon dhee**oh
112	e**katon dho**-dheka
200	dheeah-**ko**sia
300	trah-**ko**sia
400	tetra-**ko**sia
500	penda-**ko**sia
600	eksa-**ko**sia
700	eftah-**ko**sia
800	awkta-**ko**sia
900	enaya-**ko**sia
1000	**hee**lia
2000	**dhee**oh heeliah-dhess
10,000	**dhe**ka heeliah-dhess
50,000	pe**neen**da heeliah-dhess
100,000	e**katon** heeliah-dhess
1999	**hee**lia enaya-**ko**sia ene**neen**da enaya
1,000,000	**ena** ekaton-**mee**rio
2,000,000	**dhee**oh ekatoh-**mee**ria
first	**pro**toh
second	**dhef**teroh
third	**tree**toh
fourth	te**tar**tos
tenth	**dheka**tos
once	**mee**a fora
twice	**dhee**o foress
three times	treess foress

one-quarter	**ena tetartoh**
one-half	**meeso**
three-quarters	**treeah tetarta**
one-third	**ena treetoh**
two-thirds	**dheeoh treeta**

30. WEIGHTS & MEASURES

In Greece, virtually all solids and liquids are sold by kilos and grams, by their weight rather than volume. The single exception is gasoline, which is sold by the liter.

kilometer	heelioh-metro
(kilometers	heelioh-metra)
meter	**metro**
(meters	**metra**}
gallon	galonee
(gallons	galonia)
liter	**leetroh**
(liters	**leetra**)
kilo	keela
(kilos	keela)
gram	gram**ario**
(grams	gram**aria**)

31. OPPOSITES

beginning - end	arhee - telos
clean - dirty	katharo - vromiko
comfortable - uncomfortable	ahnetoh - ahvolo
happy - unhappy	efteek-hees-menos - dhees-teek-hees-menos
life - death	zoee - thanatos
friend - enemy	feelos - ekhthros
modern - traditional	modherna - para-dho-siakos
modern - ancient	modherna - arhayo
open - shut	ahneektoh - kleestoh
wide - narrow	far-dhee - stenoh
high - low	pseela - hameelo
peace - war	eereenee - polemos
polite - rude	evyenikos - ah-yenees
silence - noise	see-opee - thorivos
cheap - expensive	f-theeno - ah-krivo
hot/warm - cold/cool	zestoh - kreeoh
health - disease	eegyeeah - ahrostia
well - sick	eeg-yee-ees - ahrostos
night - day	neekta - mehra
top - bottom	ehpano - katoh
backwards - forwards	pros ta peeso - embros
back - front	peeso - brosta
dead - alive	nekros - zo-danos
near - far	konda - mah-kreeah
left - right	ahreestehra - dheksiah
in - out	mehsa - ekso
up - down	ehpano - katoh
yes - no	nay - oh-hee

here - there	ehdho - ekkee
soft - hard	malako - skleero
easy - difficult	efkolo - **dhees**kolo
quick - slow	**greego**ra - seega
big - small	**megah**lo - meekro
old - young	yehros - **neh**-os
tall - short	pseelos - kondohs
strong - weak	dheenatohs - ah-**dhee**natos
success - failure	epiteeheea - ahpoteeheea
new - old	**neh**-os - paliohs
question - answer	roteesi - ah**pahn**disi
safety - danger	ahsfalia - **keen**-dheenos
good - bad	kalo - kako
true - false	ahleethino - pseftiko
light - heavy	elafro - vahree
light *noun* - dark *noun*	fohs - skota-dhee
well - badly	kala - kakos
truth - lie	ahleethia - psema

32. GREEK PLACE NAMES

Where is...?	Poo eenay...?
How far is...?	Poso mahkriah eenay...?
Is there a ship (train/bus) for...?	Ekhee pleeo (trayno/leh-oforeeo) ya...?

Acropolis, the	ee Ah-kropolees
Aegean, the	ee Ayg-**yay**-on
Aegina	Ay**gyee**na
Athens	Ah**thee**na
Attica	Ah**ti**kee
Boetia	Vee-o**tee**a
Cephalonia	Kefa**lo**niah
Chalkidiki	Halki-**dhi**kee
Chania	Hah**niah**
Chios	**Hee**ohs
Corfu	**Kehr**keera
Corinth	Ko**reen**thos
Crete	**Kree**tee
Cyclades	Kee**kla**-dhess
Delos	**Dhee**los
Delphi	Dhel-**fee**
Dodecanese	Dho-dheh-**kah**-neesa
Epidauros	Eh**pee**-dhavros
Epirus	**Ee**peeros
Euboea	E**vee**a
Herakleion	Ee**rah**klio
Hydra	**Ee**-dhra
Igoumenitsa	Eegoo-me**nee**tsa
Ionion Islands	Neesiah tou Ee-oh**nee**oo
Ios	**Ee**ohs
Ithaca	Ee**tha**kee

Knossos	Kno**sohs**
Lesbos	**Les**vos
Macedonia	Mahke-dhon**eea**
Meteora	Meh**teh**-ora
Mt. Athos	**Ahyon Oros**
Mt. Lycabettus	**Oros** Leekav**eetohs**
Mt. Olympus	**Oros Ohleempos**
Mt. Pelion	**Oros Pee**lion
Mycenae	Mee**kee**nay
Mykonos	**Mee**konos
Mytelene	Meetee**lee**nee
Naupactus	**Nahf**paktohs
Naxos	**Nahk**sos
Olympia	Ohleem**beea**
Paros	**Pah**ros
Parthenon	**Par**thenon
Patmos	**Paht**mos
Patras	**Pah**tras
Peloponnese	Peloponisos
Phaestos	Fay**stos**
Philippi	**Fee**lipee
Piraeus	Pee**ra**yefs
Poros	**Poros**
Rethymnon	**Retheem**non
Rhodes	**Ro**-dhohs
Samos	**Sah**mos
Samothrace	Samo**thra**kee
Santorini	Santo**ree**nee or **Thee**ra
Saronic Gulf	**Kol**pos tou Saroni**kou**
Serifos	**Seh**rifos
Sifnos	**Seef**nos
Skiathos	Skee**ah**thos
Skopelos	**Sko**pelos

Skyros	**Skee**ros
Souda	**Soo**-dha
Sounion	**Soo**nion
Sparta	**Spar**ti
Spetsai	**Spet**sess
Thasos	**Tha**sos
Thebes	**Thee**vay
Thera	**Thee**ra
Thermopylae	Thehrmo**pee**lay
Thessaloniki	Thessalo**nee**kee
Thessaly	Thessa**lee**a
Thrace	**Thra**kee
Tinos	**Tee**nos
Volos	**Vo**los
Vouliagmeni	Vooliahg**me**nee
Yannina	Yoah**nee**na
Zakynthos	**Zah**keenthos

FURTHER READING

For general reading regarding the history and culture of Greece, there are two relatively short paperback volumes which provide good, inexpensive, intelligent and entertaining looks at the country: A.R Burns' *Penguin History of Greece* and Richard Clogg's *A Concise History of Greece*. The former concentrates on the pre-Christian era while the latter is very good about more recent events. For specialized reading, Robert Graves' *Greek Myths* remains unparalleled in that area, while *The Oxford History of the Classical World*, ed. By John Boardman, and Donald Kagan's four-volume study of the Peloponnesian Wars wonderfully illuminate the rise and fall of Classical Athens, before, during and after. The most highly recommended studies of Alexander the Great are those by Peter Green and Robin Lane Fox, while *A Short History of Byzantium* by John Julius Norwich deals in riveting fashion with the next great age of Greece and the beginnings of its Christian era. As noted above, Richard Clogg's history makes good sense out of the tortuous evolution of modern Greece since the revolution against the Ottoman Empire, but for a deeper personal look at the anguish it has encompassed, read Nicholas Gage's *Eleni*, which deals with the civil strife following World War II, and Oriana Fallaci's *A Man*, which tells of her passionate romantic involvement with one of the great martyrs of the resistance against the Colonel's junta in the late 1960's and early 1970's. Finally, for a look at just about everything else you might want to know about Greece but may be afraid to ask, try this author's *The Essential Greek Handbook: An A to Z Phrasal Guide* published by Hippocrene Books.

ATHENS:
SINTAGMA (CONSTITUTION SQUARE)

1. Sintagma
2. To and from Piraeus and the Acropolis
3. To Plaka
4. To Plaka, Monastiraki Flea Market, subway.
5. From Monastiraki and Piraeus
6. From Omonia Square
7. To Omonia Square, subway, Piraeus
8. From Kaningos Square
9. To Kolonaki Square and Mt. Lycabettus
10. To and from: American & British Embassies, the Megaron, and the Hilton Hotel & Athens Tower

A. Parliament Building
B. Airport Bus Stop Terminal
C. Motor Insurance Bureau
D. Luggage depot, Pacific Ltd., 24 & 26 Nikis St.
E. Central Post Office
F. American Express
G. Bookstore
H. Tourist Bureau (E.O.T.)
I. Telephone & Telegraph Office
J. Bookstore
K. Book & Magazine store

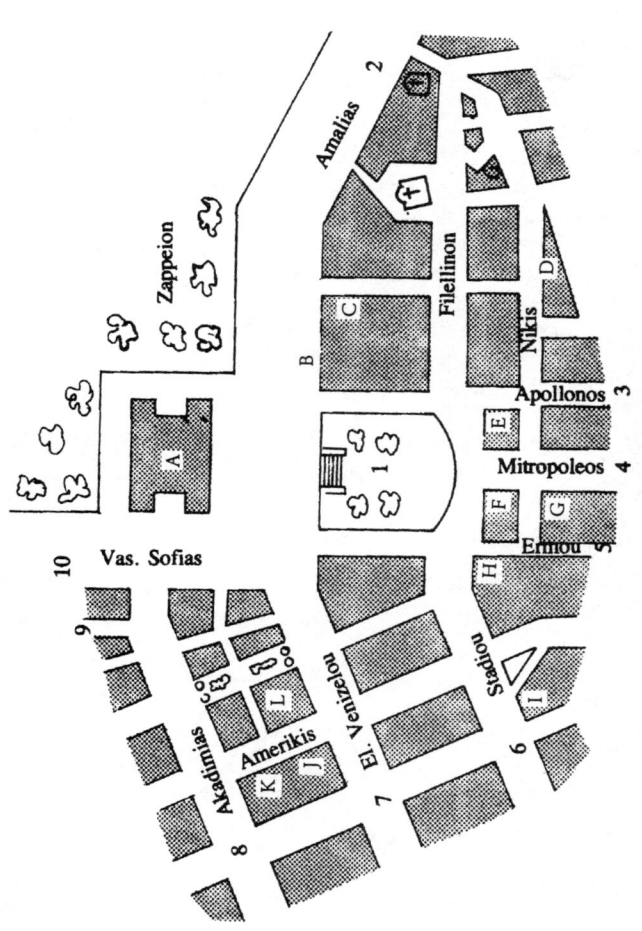

PIRAEUS

1. Karaiskakis Square
2. Travel agencies, boat tickets
3 & 3a. Boats to the Aegean Islands
4. Boats to the Saronic Islands
5 & 5a. Boats to Crete
6. Foreign ships: arrivals and departures

A. Customs House
B. Subway Station to Athens; Telephone & Telegraph Office
C. Trains to the Peloponnese
D. Trains to northern Greece
E. Tourist Police, 43 Akti Miaoulis

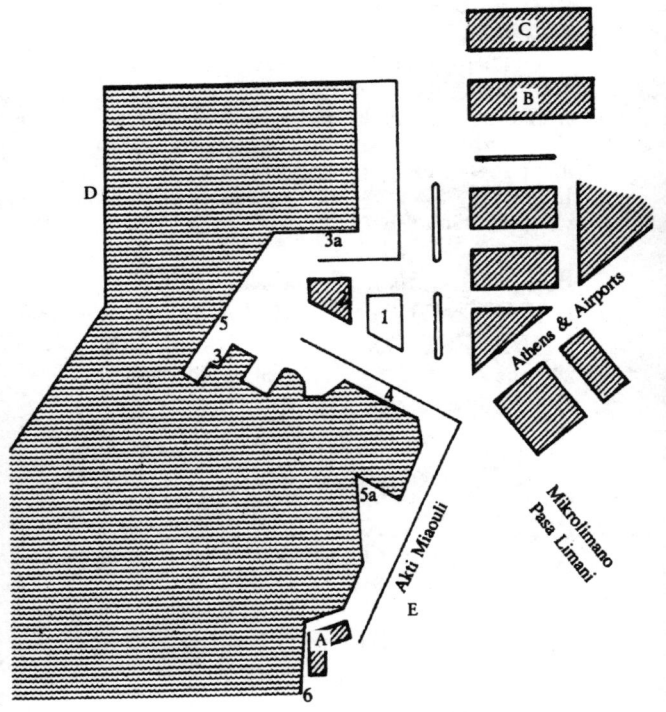

DICTIONARY & PHRASEBOOK SERIES

AUSTRALIAN DICTIONARY AND PHRASEBOOK
Helen Jonsen

Displaying the diversity of English, this book provides terms connected with specific situations such as driving, size conversion charts, travel options, and sightseeing trips are just a few of the many topics provided.

131 pages • 3¾ x 7 • 1,500 entries • 0-7818-0539-2 • W • $11.95pb • (626)

BASQUE-ENGLISH/ENGLISH-BASQUE DICTIONARY AND PHRASEBOOK

240 pages • 3¾ x 7 • 1,500 entries • 0-7818-0622-4 • W • $11.95pb

BOSNIAN-ENGLISH/ENGLISH-BOSNIAN DICTIONARY AND PHRASEBOOK

175 pages • 3¾ x 7 • 1,500 entries • 0-7818-0596-1 • W • $11.95pb • (691)

BRETON-ENGLISH/ENGLISH-BRETON DICTIONARY AND PHRASEBOOK

131 pages • 3¾ x 7 • 1,500 entries • 0-7818-0540-6 • W • $11.95pb • (627)

BRITISH-AMERICAN/AMERICAN-BRITISH DICTIONARY AND PHRASEBOOK

160 pages • 3¾ x 7 • 1,400 entries • 0-7818-0450-7 • W • $11.95pb • (247)

CHECHEN-ENGLISH/ENGLISH-CHECHEN DICTIONARY AND PHRASEBOOK
160 pages • 3¾ x 7 • 1,400 entries • 0-7818-0446-9 • NA • $11.95pb • (183)

GEORGIAN-ENGLISH/ENGLISH-GEORGIAN DICTIONARY AND PHRASEBOOK
150 pages • 3¾ x 7 • 1,300 entries • 0-7818-0542-2 • W • $11.95pb • (630)

IRISH-ENGLISH/ENGLISH-IRISH DICTIONARY AND PHRASEBOOK
160 pages • 3¾ x 7 • 1,400 entries/phrases • 0-87052-110-1 • NA • $7.95pb • (385)

LINGALA-ENGLISH/ENGLISH-LINGALA DICTIONARY AND PHRASEBOOK
120 pages • 3¾ x 7 • 0-7818-0456-6 • W • $11.95pb • (296)

MALTESE-ENGLISH/ENGLISH-MALTESE DICTIONARY AND PHRASEBOOK
175 pages 3¾ x 7 • 1,500 entries • 0-7818-0565-1 • W • $11.95pb • (697)

POLISH DICTIONARY AND PHRASEBOOK
252 pages • 5½ x 8½ • 0-7818-0134-6 • W • $11.95pb • (192)
Cassettes—Vol I: 0-7818-0340-3 • W • $12.95 • (492)
Vol II: 0-7818-0384-5 • W • $12.95 • (486)

RUSSIAN DICTIONARY AND PHRASEBOOK, *Revised*
256pages • 5½ x 8½ • 3,000 entries • 0-7818-0190-7 • W • $9.95pb • (597)

UKRAINIAN DICTIONARY AND PHRASEBOOK
205 pages • 5½ x 8½ • 3,000 entries • 0-7818-0188-5 • W • $11.95pb • (28)

Hippocrene's Beginner's Series...

Do you know what it takes to make a phone call in Russia? Or how to get through customs in Japan? This new language instruction series shows how to handle oneself in typical situations by introducing the business person or traveler not only to the vocabulary, grammar, and phrases of a new language, but also the history, customs, and daily practices of a foreign country.

The Beginner's Series consists of basic language instruction, which also includes vocabulary, grammar, and common phrases and review questions, along with cultural insights, interesting historical background, the country's basic facts and hints about everyday living-driving, shopping, eating out, and more.

Arabic For Beginners
186 pages • 5¼ x 8¼ • 0-7818-01141 • $9.95pb • (18)

Beginner's Assyrian
185 pages • 5 x 9 • 0-7818-0677-1 • $11.95pb • (763)

Beginner's Chinese
150 pages • 5½ x 8 • 0-7818-0566-x • $14.95pb • (690)

Beginner's Bulgarian
207 pages • 5½ x 8½ • 0-7818-0300-4 • $9.95pb • (76)

Beginner's Czech
200 pages • 5½ x 8½ • 0-7818-0231-8 • $9.95pb • (74)

Beginner's Esperanto
400 pages • 5½ x 8½ • 0-7818-0230-x • $14.95pb • (51)

Beginner's Hungarian
200 pages • 5½ x 7 • 0-7818-0209-1 • $7.95pb • (68)

Beginner's Japanese
200 pages • 5½ x 8½ • 0-7818-0234-2 • $11.95pb • (53)

Beginner's Lithuanian
230 pages • 6 x 9 • 0-7818-0678-X • $14.95pb • (764)

Beginner's Maori
121 pages • 5½ x 8½ • 0-7818-0605-4 • $8.95pb • (703)

Beginner's Persian
150 pages • 5½ x 8 • 0-7818-0567-8 • $14.95pb • (696)

Beginner's Polish
200 pages • 5½ x 8½ • 0-7818-0299-7 • $9.95pb • (82)

Beginner's Romanian
200 pages • 5½ x 8½ • 0-7818-0208-3 • $7.95pb • (79)

Beginner's Russian
200 pages • 5½ x 8½ • 0-7818-0232-6 • $9.95pb • (61)

Beginner's Swahili
200 pages • 5½ x 8½ • 0-7818-0335-7 • $9.95pb • (52)

Beginner's Ukrainian
130 pages • 5½ x 8½ • 0-7818-0443-4 • $11.95pb • (88)

Beginner's Vietnamese
517 pages • 7 x 10 • 30 lessons • 0-7818-0411-6 • $19.95pb • (253)

Beginner's Welsh
210 pages • 5½ x 8½ • 0-7818-0589-9 • $9.95pb • (712)

About out Mastering Series...

These imaginative courses, designed for both individual and classroom use, assume no previous knowledge of the language. The unique combination of practical exercises and step-by-step grammar emphasizes a functional approach to new scripts and their vocabularies. Everyday situations and local customs are explored variously through dialogues, newspaper extracts, drawings and photos. Cassettes are available for each language.

MASTERING ARABIC
320 pages • 5¼ x 8¼ • 0-87052-922-6 • USA • $14.95pb • (501)
2 cassettes: 0-87052-984-6 • (507)

MASTERING FINNISH
278 pages • 5½ x 8½ • 0-7818-0233-4 • W • $14.95pb • (184)
2 Cassettes: 0-7818-0265-2 • W • $12.95 • (231)

MASTERING FRENCH
288 pages • 5½ x 8½ • 0-87052-055-5 USA • $14.95pb • (511)
2 Cassettes: • 0-87052-060-1 USA • $12.95 • (512)

MASTERING ADVANCED FRENCH
348 pages • 5½ x 8½ • 0-7818-0312-8 • W • $14.95pb • (41)
2 Cassettes: • 0-7818-0313-6 • W • $12.95 • (54)

MASTERING GERMAN
340 pages • 5½ x 8½ • 0-87052-056-3 • USA • $11.95pb • (514)
2 Cassettes: • 0-87052-061-X USA • $12.95 • (515)

MASTERING ITALIAN
360 pages • 5½ x 8½ • 0-87052-057-1 • USA • $11.95pb • (517)
2 Cassettes: 0-87052-066-0 • USA • $12.95 • (521)

MASTERING ADVANCED ITALIAN
278 pages • 5½ x 8½ • 0-7818-0333-0 • W • $14.95pb • (160)
2 Cassettes: 0-7818-0334-9 • W • $12.95 • (161)

MASTERING JAPANESE
368 pages • 5½ x 8½ • 0-87052-923-4 • USA • $14.95pb • (523)
2 Cassettes: • 0-87052-983-8 • USA • $12.95 • (524)

MASTERING NORWEGIAN
183 pages • 5½ x 8½ • 0-7818-0320-9 • W • $14.95pb • (472)

MASTERING POLISH
288 pages • 5½ x 8½ • 0-7818-0015-3 • W • $14.95pb • (381)
2 Cassettes: • 0-7818-0016-1 • W • $12.95 • (389)

MASTERING RUSSIAN
278 pages • 5½ x 8½ • 0-7818-0270-9 • W • $14.95pb • (11)
2 Cassettes: • 0-7818-0271-7 • W • $12.95 • (13)

MASTERING SPANISH
338 pages • 5½ x 8½ • 0-87052-059-8 USA • $11.95 • (527)
2 Cassettes: • 0-87052-067-9 USA • $12.95 • (528)

MASTERING ADVANCED SPANISH
326 pp • 5½ x 8½ • 0-7818-0081-1 • W • $14.95pb • (413)
2 Cassettes: • 0-7818-0089-7 • W • $12.95 • (426)

Practical Dictionaries From Hippocrene:

AFRIKAANS-ENGLISH/ENGLISH-AFRIKAANS PRACTICAL DICTIONARY
430 pages • 4½ x 6½ • 14,000 entries • 0-7818-0052-8 • NA • (134)

ALBANIAN-ENGLISH/ENGLISH-ALBANIAN PRACTICAL DICTIONARY
400 pages • 4⅜ x 7 • 18,000 entries • 0-7818-0419-1 • W except Albania • $14.95pb • (483)

BULGARIAN-ENGLISH/ENGLISH-BULGARIAN PRACTICAL DICTIONARY
323 pages • 4⅜ x 7 • 6,500 entries • 0-87052-145-4 • NA • $14.95pb • (331)

DANISH-ENGLISH/ENGLISH-DANISH PRACTICAL DICTIONARY
601 pages • 4⅜ x 7 • 32,000 entries • 0-7818-0823-8 • NA • $14.95pb • (198)

FRENCH-ENGLISH/ ENGLISH-FRENCH PRACTICAL DICTIONARY,
with larger print
386 pages • 5½ x 8¼ • 35,000 entries • 0-7818-355-1 • W • $9.95pb • (499)

FULANI-ENGLISH PRACTICAL DICTIONARY
264 pages • 5 x 7¼ • 0-7818-0404-3 • W • $14.95pb • (38)

GERMAN-ENGLISH/ENGLISH-GERMAN PRACTICAL DICTIONARY, *with larger print*
400 pages • 5½ x 8¼ • 35,000 entries • 0-7818-355-1 • W • $9.95pb • (200)

HINDI-ENGLISH/ ENGLISH-HINDI PRACTICAL DICTIONARY
745 pages • 4³⁄₈ x 7 • 25,000 entries • 0-7818-0084-6 • W • $19.95pb • (442)

ENGLISH-HINDI PRACTICAL DICTIONARY
399 pages • 4³⁄₈ x 7 • 15,000 entries • 0-87052-978-1 • NA • $11.95pb • (362)

INDONESIAN-ENGLISH/ENGLISH-INDONESIAN PRACTICAL DICTIONARY
289 pages • 4¼ x 7 • 17,000 entries • 0-87052-810-6 • NA • $11.95pb • (127)

ITALIAN-ENGLISH/ENGLISH-ITALIAN PRACTICAL DICTIONARY,
with larger print
488 pages • 5½ x 8¼ • 35,000 entries • 0-7818-354-3 • W • $9.95p • (201)

KOREAN-ENGLISH/ENGLISH-KOREAN PRACTICAL DICTIONARY
365 pages • 4 x 7¼ • 8,500 entries • 0-87052-092-x • Asia and NA • $14.95pb • (399)

LATVIAN-ENGLISH/ENGLISH-LATVIAN PRACTICAL DICTIONARY
474 pages • 4³/₈ x 7 • 16,000 entries • 0-7818-0059-5
• NA • $16.95pb • (194)

POLISH-ENGLISH/ENGLISH-POLISH PRACTICAL DICTIONARY
703 pages • 5¼ x 8½ • 31,000 entries • 0-7818-085-4
• W • $11.95pb • (450)

SERBO-CROATIAN-ENGLISH/ENGLISH-SERBO-CROATIAN PRACTICAL DICTIONARY
400 pages • 5³/₈ x 7 • 24,000 entries • 0-7818-0445-0
• W • $16.95pb • (130)

UKRAINIAN-ENGLISH/ENGLISH-UKRAINIAN PRACTICAL DICTIONARY, *Revised edition with menu terms*
406 pages • 4¼ x 7 • 16,000 entries • 0-7818-0306-3
• W • $14.95pb • (343)

YIDDISH-ENGLISH/ ENGLISH-YIDDISH PRACTICAL DICTIONARY, Expanded edition
215 pages • 4½ x 7 • 4,000 entries • 0-7818-0439-6
• W • $9.95pb • (431)

All prices are subject to change. To order Hippocrene Books, contact your local bookstore, call (718) 454-2366, or write to : Hippocrene Books, 171 Madison Ave. New York, NY 10016. Please enclose check or money order adding $5.00 shipping (UPS) for the first book and $.50 for each additional title.